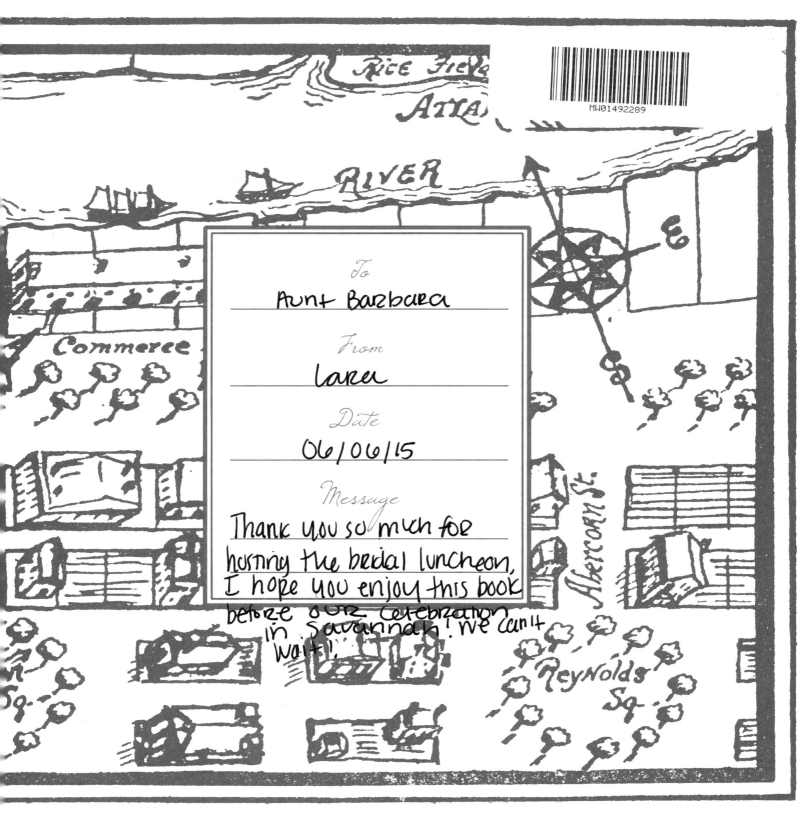

On the SQUARES
Savannah Style

JUNIOR LEAGUE OF SAVANNAH
Women building better communities

FOREWORD
Damon Lee Fowler

COPYWRITERS
Kathy Ledvina
Catherine Edwards
Katie Joyner

PHOTOGRAPHY
Katie Joyner

EDITORS
Nelle Bordeaux
Catherine Edwards

On the SQUARES
Savannah Style

A COOKBOOK CELEBRATING GEORGIA'S FIRST CITY

JUNIOR LEAGUE OF SAVANNAH
Women building better communities

Published by The Junior League of Savannah, Inc.

Copyright © 2015 by The Junior league of Savannah, Inc.

P.O. Box 23545, Savannah, Georgia 31403
912-790-1002

www.jrleaguesav.org

Cover, food and chapter opener photography
© by Katie Joyner

Cover Image: Orleans Square

Back Cover Images: Beef Tenderloin Bruschetta, Monterey Square, Palmetto Pink Cake, Grilled Corn and Tomato Summer Salad

ISBN: 978-0-9613411-2-1   LCCN: 2015931333

Additional copies of *On the Squares – Savannah Style* may be obtained by writing or calling The Junior League of Savannah, Inc., P.O. Box 23545, Savannah, Georgia 31403, 912-790-1002, www.jrleaguesav.org, headquarters@jrleaguesav.org

All proceeds from the sale of *On the Squares—Savannah Style* will benefit the community and the charitable activities of The Junior League of Savannah, Inc.

Favorite Recipes® Press

SOUTHWESTERN Publishing Group, Inc.

www.frpbooks.com   www.swpublishinggroup.com
P. O. Box 305142, Nashville Tennessee 37230
1-800-358-0560

ACKNOWLEDGMENTS

On the Squares—Savannah Style has been produced by the Junior League of Savannah, Inc.'s, active and sustaining members with their contributions of more than 500 recipes for testing and tasting. Thank you to Mary Kerdasha for putting in the time and effort to research and launch the beginning stages of this book; Rosanne Perna for administrative support; Stephanie Meredith for getting the ball rolling and starting the process of assembling recipes and helping to create the perfect name for this book; Kathy Ledvina for working countless hours on organizing and writing the historical copy that is depicted in each chapter opener; Nelle Bordeaux for help with editing copy and researching historical League documents; the Georgia Historical Society for use of its collection of the Junior League of Savannah's archival photos; the Wilkes family for permission to include the Wilkes Boarding House meat loaf recipe; and our 2013–2015 New Cookbook Committees for going over and beyond the call of voluntarism to help create a masterpiece.

Katie Joyner, *Chair*

Catherine Edwards, *Recipe Director and Co-Chair*

2014–2015 NEW COOKBOOK COMMITTEE

Amy Riesinger, *President*

Katie Joyner, *Chair*

Catherine Edwards, *Co-Chair*

Carey Ford

Hilary Parry

Rebecca Strawn

2013–2014 NEW COOKBOOK COMMITTEE

Nelle Bordeaux, *President*

Katie Joyner, *Chair*

Catherine Edwards, *Co-Chair*

Carey Ford

Kathy Ledvina

Victoria Mathews

Lisa Muller

Hilary Parry

Samantha Pogorelsky

Jenny Rutherford

Rebecca Strawn

MISSION

The Junior League of Savannah, Inc., was established on January 7, 1926 to further interest among its members in social, economic, educational, cultural, and civic conditions of the community through effective volunteer service. Through the power of the association, the Junior League of Savannah strengthens communities by embracing diverse perspectives, building partnerships, and inspiring shared solutions.

The Junior League of Savannah is an organization of women committed to promoting voluntarism, developing the potential of women, and improving communities through the effective action and leadership of trained volunteers. Its purpose is exclusively educational and charitable. Members have given millions of volunteer hours and more than $3 million to the community. We are proud to have impacted Savannah and the surrounding communities for 90 years.

The Junior League of Savannah is part of the Association of Junior Leagues International, Inc.

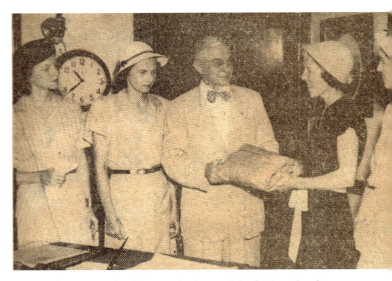

Savannah's mayor, John G. Kennedy, donated the first bundle of clothing for the 1947 Junior League of Savannah's Thrift Sale. The Junior League volunteers went to the mayor's office in city hall to collect this first donation.

FOREWORD

It's often said that Savannahians don't like change and are slow to accept it. The punch line to the joke about how many Savannahians it takes to change a light bulb, delivered in a tone of shock, is, "CHANGE?!"

The joke does resonate with a kernel of truth: The architecture, streets, and squares of our historic downtown would certainly not have been so carefully preserved had Savannah not been slow to accept change for change's sake. However, a stroll down any block of that same downtown, where time-worn brick and stucco rub elbows with sleek, polished plate glass and steel, gives away another side of the city. While Savannah clearly reveres its past, it has embraced the modern world—and done so with the same grace and style that saw our ancestors through nearly three centuries of war, plague, enemy invasion, and economic upheaval.

It isn't just in its public streets and squares that Savannah's past coexists with the modern world: we find the same blending of old and new in our kitchens and on our tables. The legendary cooking and hospitality that long ago earned Savannah its reputation as "The Hostess City" remains strong and embodies still the grace and style of its past. But while the food that comes from our kitchens today is sometimes still served on linen-draped tables and illuminated by silver candelabra, it's informed and even transformed by the realities of modern life.

Formal dinners with a dozen courses have given way to cocktail parties with a dozen appetizers; in all but a very few homes, the breadwinners are also the cooks. Technology, economics, immigration, and a growing interest in international cooking have all played a hand in what we stir into the pot—not to mention who is doing the stirring. And yet, through it all, Savannah's cooking has remained rooted in its history and has its own unique flair.

Since the publication of the timeless classic *Savannah Style* in 1980, the delicious legacy of that unique cuisine has been in the capable hands of the Junior League of Savannah. Not only did their book capture Savannah's unique brand of hospitality, thirty-plus years later, it's still in print, giving testament to the fact that real style never goes out of fashion. Since then, two things have not changed: Savannah's love of good food and of sharing it generously, and the Junior League's commitment to simplicity that doesn't compromise quality or elegance.

In the introduction to that first volume we read that "this book is written for busy, active people who still care about graceful living and stylish entertaining, but who must accomplish it with less help than our forebears." That same spirit inspires and informs this new collection. The recipes you will find here celebrate the kitchens of our past but embrace our present, reflecting the best of how we cook, entertain, and nourish our families today—simply, elegantly, and always with a touch of that unique, inimitable Savannah style.

— *Damon Lee Fowler*

CONTENTS

opposite page: Spanish moss drapes the trees in Oglethorpe Square.

INTRODUCTION

Savannah's squares have always been the most distinctive feature of the "Hostess City of the South." Various public activities, entertainment, and celebrations took place in the squares when they were first established, and the same is true today. Along with the festivities, each Savannah square was shaped by Georgia's developing history. The city's squares, wards, parks, streets, monuments, and plaques are all physical eulogies to the perseverance of the heroic persons in our history. The twenty-four original Savannah squares bear witness to Savannah's transformation into a world-class city also known as the First City—the first city founded in the state of Georgia.

Savannah's design is unique. A harmonious and graceful union of the old and new preserve Savannah's graces. We hope this book showcases not only Savannah's charm, but also a taste of our coastal Southern cuisine. With more than 140 triple-tested recipes, this cookbook will be a companion piece to our two legacy cookbooks, *Savannah Style* and *Downtown Savannah Style.* This new book features the history of Savannah's squares and includes delicious modern dishes accented with cooking tips, beverages, and condiment accompaniments, as well as some of the Junior League of Savannah's own history. Our history as an organization parallels the history of the city and region we seek to serve.

above: Troup Square's Armillary Sphere.
opposite page: Spring azaleas blooming in Chatham Square.

SAVANNAH'S CITY PLAN

General James Edward Oglethorpe and 35 families arrived at Yamacraw Bluff in early February 1733 to establish Savannah, the capital of the new Georgia colony. Within months Oglethorpe advised the first colonists of his plan for the settlement of Georgia, assigned names, and allocated lots at the site of present-day Savannah. Oglethorpe's original plan designated squares as the center of each divided district described as a "ward". The original four wards were named after four prominent Georgia Trustees: Percival, Heathcote, Derby, and Decker.

Each square had two large "trust" lots flanking the east and west sides, initially reserved by the colony's trustees for public buildings, churches, or institutions. As the city expanded, prominent citizens were awarded these lots.

The northern and southern sides of the square were divided into four "tithings", each separated by a lane. The tithing (or tything) blocks were then divided into ten individual lots measuring roughly 60 x 90 feet, reserved for residential use. The center square served multiple purposes for the inhabitants of the surrounding building: pasture land, parade ground, and protection from fires and attack. In addition to the town lot, each freeholder (male inhabitant of majority age) was allotted a five-acre garden lot and a farm of around forty-five acres, for a total of 50 acres. Today the success of Oglethorpe's city plan is heralded as being ahead of its time and is used as a model for modern urban planning.

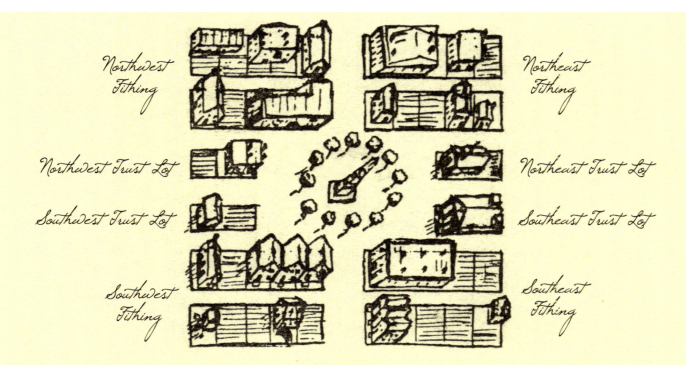

Northwest Tithing

Northeast Tithing

Northwest Trust Lot

Northeast Trust Lot

Southwest Trust Lot

Southeast Trust Lot

Southwest Tithing

Southeast Tithing

CITY OF SAVANNAH MAP

1   Johnson Square

2   Wright Square

3   Chippewa Square

4   Madison Square

5   Monterey Square

6-1 Ellis Square

6-2 Telfair Square

6-3 Reynolds Square

6-4 Oglethorpe Square

7-1 Warren Square

7-2 Washington Square

7-3 Columbia Square

7-4 Greene Square

8-1 Crawford Square

8-2 Troup Square

8-3 Whitefield Square

8-4 Calhoun Square

8-5 Lafayette Square

9-1 Franklin Square

9-2 Orleans Square

9-3 Pulaski Square

9-4 Chatham Square

*Numbers above
indicate the square's
location and
chapter in which
it is introduced.*

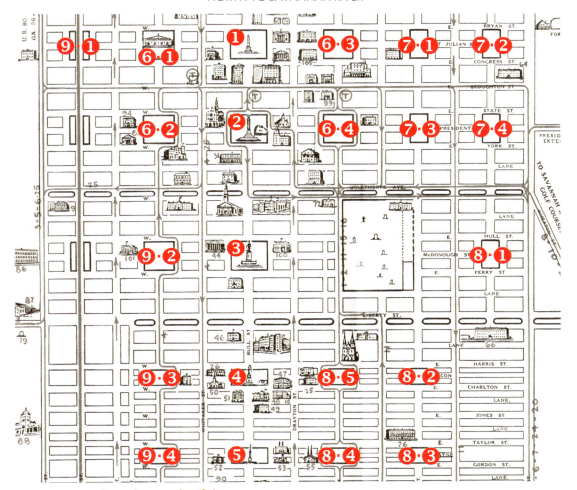

NORTH TO SAVANNAH RIVER

savannah's hospitality

When Savannah was founded, it was "under sever penalty all brandies and distilled liquors were prohibited." It was not until 1750 that the House of Commons voted to repeal the act. It soon became customary that when a neighbor or stranger approached the house, his horse was taken to the stable, saddlebags taken into the house, and the guest immediately escorted to the sideboard and invited to take a drink from the various liquors displayed. So universal was the custom that if this invitation were not extended, it was considered a breach in hospitality.

BULL STREET PROMENADE

On February 9, 1733, James E. Oglethorpe and Colonel William Bull marked out Savannah's first squares, lots, and streets, and colonists started construction on Savannah's clapboard cottages. In tribute to the generosity of South Carolina's citizens, several Savannah streets bear their names; however, Savannah's most distinguished principal promenade honors the Royal Governor of South Carolina, Colonel William Bull.

In 1799, the City Exchange was constructed, and by 1812 Bull Street became home to Savannah's first permanent site of government. The Exchange building was replaced in 1905 by the dome of Savannah's City Hall. This gilded structure at the corner of Bull and Bay streets marks the start of the most central, handsome, and fashionable street in Savannah.

The squares along the Bull Street promenade are favored by residents and tourists alike. Bull Street squares were the first to have monuments, electric light towers, and formal landscaped walks, necessitating the removal of the city's firehouses and water pumps from the squares.

By 1876, a city ordinance required these squares to be enclosed to keep out transients and livestock. Around most squares, horizontal wood fences with turnstile entrances were erected; the Bull Street squares were surrounded by decorative iron railings. It soon proved that these barriers were expensive to maintain and provided both a roosting place for young boys and protection for goats and cows herded inside for late-night grazing. The city soon removed all fences from around the squares and installed granite curbing. Only the iron fences around Pulaski and the Confederate Monuments remain in place. The iron railing that enclosed Johnson Square was purchased by the church congregation and re-erected on the west and south sides of the Cathedral of St. John the Baptist.

Today, Savannah's grand Bull Street promenade, from City Hall to Forsyth Park, features some of Savannah's finest architecture, historic artifacts, and markers. The squares along its path are the most prominent in Savannah, with iconic imagery that has come to represent the city. Transecting downtown, Bull Street's restored monuments reach skyward and commemorate our most esteemed citizens, whose leadership and sacrifice significantly changed the course of Savannah's history. Lining the street are outstanding architectural gems designed by Savannah's first and finest architects, including Charles B. Cluskey, William Jay, John S. Norris, William Preston, and Henrik Wallin.

opposite page: Camellia blossoms are lovely spots of color in Monterey Square.

APPETIZERS

JOHNSON SQUARE, DERBY WARD—1733

After fifty-five days at sea, Oglethorpe and the 125 "sober, moral, and industrious" colonists who arrived aboard the frigate *Ann* were welcomed and supported by South Carolina Governor Robert Johnson. Savannah's first square, laid out in 1733, honored Johnson's hospitality and quickly established its role in Savannah's history as the central square of colonial life. Johnson Square was surrounded by the House for Strangers, the Public Mill, the Public Bake Oven, the Public Store, and nearby the Public Well. In the center, a large sundial was erected on which the colonists read the time of day. Home to Oglethorpe's original tent from which the city was governed, Johnson Square is also the site of Christ Episcopal Church, where services were established in 1733. The town's first forty clapboard houses were built near Johnson Square.

Known as the Forest City, Savannah values planting and protecting its abundance of trees. Care of Savannah's squares, streets, and lanes has been a city priority since 1810. Johnson Square was the first to be beautified in order to provide a picturesque setting for William Strickland's 1930 obelisk commemorating General Nathanael Greene, second in command and a distinguished Revolutionary War hero. The cornerstone was laid by his comrade-in-arms, General Lafayette, in the Masonic tradition, by pouring corn, wine, and oil from gold and silver vessels on the structure when he visited the city in 1825. Finished in 1829, the marble shaft is Savannah's oldest monument.

Johnson Square continues to maintain its dominance as the heart of commercial Savannah and is surrounded by Savannah's earliest institutions and some of the city's first skyscrapers.

Even the challenge of a nation at war did not stop the Junior League of Savannah! The Junior League of Savannah's Thrift Sale began in November 1947 and had a net profit of $1,610. Here, member Mrs. W. T. Knight, III gathers items for the Thrift Sale.

opposite page: Savannah's oldest monument is found in Johnson Square.

Beef Tenderloin Bruschetta

ingredients

2 or 3 (12-inch) baguettes

Extra-virgin olive oil for drizzling
    and tossing

3 pounds beef tenderloin (see page 112)

6 yellow and/or red plum tomatoes
    (or substitute equal weight of
    grape tomatoes)

4 garlic cloves

¼ cup fresh basil

¼ cup fresh tarragon, or 4 teaspoons
    dried tarragon

3 shallots

1 tablespoon lemon juice

Salt and black pepper to taste

5 ounces Gorgonzola
    or other blue cheese, crumbled

directions

Slice the baguettes at a 45-degree angle into ½-inch slices. Arrange on a baking sheet and drizzle with olive oil. Toast lightly in a toaster oven or under a broiler.

Sear the tenderloin to medium rare. (See page 112 for more instructions.) Let cool, then carve into slices.

Finely chop the tomatoes, garlic, basil, tarragon and shallots. Toss with the lemon juice and olive oil in a bowl. Season with salt and pepper.

Layer each baguette slice with a slice of beef. Top with some of the tomato mixture. Sprinkle with Gorgonzola. Serve cool or warm slightly in the oven.

Makes about 48 pieces, about 20 to 25 servings.

Crab and Corn Fritters with Spicy Dipping Sauce

ingredients

SPICY DIPPING SAUCE

1 cup mayonnaise

2 green onions, thinly sliced

1 tablespoon white wine vinegar

1 tablespoon Dijon mustard

½ teaspoon ground red pepper

¼ teaspoon black pepper

1 to 2 teaspoons hot red pepper sauce

CRAB AND CORN FRITTERS

1 tablespoon butter

2 tablespoons minced shallots

3 garlic cloves, minced

2 jalapeño peppers, seeded and minced

2 cups frozen whole kernel corn, thawed

2 green onions, sliced

¾ cup all-purpose flour

1 tablespoon sugar

1 teaspoon baking powder

1 teaspoon salt

¼ teaspoon black pepper

⅛ teaspoon ground red pepper

2 large eggs, separated

¾ cup buttermilk

½ pound fresh lump crabmeat

Vegetable oil for frying

directions

For the dipping sauce, stir together all ingredients in a bowl until well blended.

For the fritters, melt the butter in a large skillet over medium heat. Add the shallots, garlic, jalapeños, corn and green onions and sauté for 5 minutes.

Combine the flour, sugar, baking powder, salt, black pepper and red pepper in a large bowl and mix well. Beat the egg yolks lightly in a separate bowl. Add the buttermilk to the yolks and mix well. Stir the buttermilk mixture and sautéed vegetables into the flour mixture. Fold in the crabmeat.

Beat the egg whites with an electric mixer on high until soft peaks form. Fold half the beaten egg whites into the crabmeat batter, and then fold in the remaining whites.

Heat 2 inches of oil in a skillet to 375 degrees. Shape 1 to 2 tablespoons of the batter into a fritter shape and drop into the hot oil 4 or 5 at a time. Cook for 3 minutes or until golden on all sides, turning once. Drain on paper towels. Serve with Spicy Dipping Sauce.

Makes 8 servings.

Cilantro-Lime Chicken Wings with Cilantro Guacamole

ingredients

CILANTRO GUACAMOLE

1 avocado

3 tablespoons chopped fresh cilantro

2 teaspoons lime juice

1 garlic clove, chopped

2 tablespoons chopped red onion

¼ teaspoon salt

⅛ teaspoon black pepper

2 tablespoons mayonnaise

5 drops Tabasco sauce

½ teaspoon Worcestershire sauce

CHICKEN AND SEASONING

2½ to 3 pounds chicken wings

Creole seasoning, black pepper, garlic powder, Tabasco sauce and balsamic vinegar to taste

MARINADE

½ cup cilantro leaves

Juice of 2 large limes

4 garlic cloves, chopped

¼ cup vegetable oil

2 tablespoons honey

2 jalapeño peppers, chopped

1 tablespoon balsamic vinegar

1 tablespoon Chipotle Tabasco sauce

½ teaspoon ground cumin

½ teaspoon red pepper

directions

For the guacamole, combine all of the guacamole ingredients in a food processor. Process until well blended and quite smooth. Spoon the guacamole into a serving bowl.

For the chicken, combine the chicken wings with the Creole seasoning, black pepper, garlic powder, Tabasco sauce and balsamic vinegar in a ziptop bag. Refrigerate for 1 hour.

For the marinade, combine all the marinade ingredients in a blender and process until smoothly blended. Pour the marinade over the wings in the bag. Refrigerate for 1½ hours. Remove the wings from the marinade. Grill or broil as desired until cooked through. Arrange the chicken wings on a serving platter. Serve with the guacamole for dipping.

Makes 15 to 20 servings.

Crispy Cheese Wafers

ingredients

1 pound sharp Cheddar cheese, shredded

16 tablespoons (2 sticks)
cold unsalted butter

1 cup chopped pecans, toasted in butter

2 cups all-purpose flour

1 tablespoon Tabasco
or other hot red pepper sauce

Sea salt and cayenne pepper to taste

directions

Put the cheese in a large bowl. Cut the butter into pieces and scatter over the cheese. Let stand to soften. Add the pecans, flour and Tabasco. Combine with an electric mixer until a dough forms.

Divide the dough into 8 pieces. Roll each into a log about 1 inch in diameter. Wrap in wax paper. Chill at least 8 hours.

Preheat the oven to 350 degrees. Cut each log into ¼-inch coins. Place on a baking sheet lined with parchment paper. Sprinkle each coin with a little sea salt and cayenne pepper to taste. Bake for 11 to 12 minutes until pale golden and just firm.

Note: This recipe doubles well and also freezes beautifully, either as logs wrapped in wax paper or as baked wafers stored in an airtight bag or other container.

Makes 20 to 30 wafers per log.

Marinated Cheese

ingredients

½ cup olive oil

½ cup white wine vinegar

3 tablespoons chopped fresh or
dried parsley

1 teaspoon sugar

¾ teaspoon dried basil

½ teaspoon salt

½ teaspoon freshly ground black pepper

3 garlic cloves, minced

1 (2-ounce) jar diced pimentos, drained

1 (8-ounce) block cream cheese, chilled

1 (8-ounce) block sharp Cheddar cheese,
chilled

Assorted crackers for serving

directions

Combine the olive oil, vinegar, parsley, sugar, basil, salt, pepper, garlic and pimentos in a bowl and mix well.

Cut each block of cheese into halves lengthwise. Cut crosswise into ¼-inch-thick slices. Arrange cheese slices in a shallow baking dish, alternating cream cheese and Cheddar cheese, standing the slices on their edges. Pour the oil mixture over the cheese.

Cover and refrigerate for at least 8 hours to marinate. Transfer the cheese slices to a serving platter, arranging in the same alternating fashion. Spoon the marinade over the cheese. Serve with assorted crackers.

Makes 12 to 16 appetizer servings.

Petite Cheese Bites

ingredients

4 cups self-rising flour

16 ounces sour cream

2 cups (8 ounces) shredded sharp
   Cheddar cheese

16 tablespoons (2 sticks) butter, melted

1 teaspoon sugar

2 teaspoons salt

directions

Preheat the oven to 425 degrees.

Combine the flour, sour cream, cheese, butter, sugar and salt in a large bowl and mix well until a dough forms. Spray mini muffin cups with butter-flavor nonstick cooking spray. Fill cups to the top with the batter. Bake for 15 minutes.

Makes 24 to 36 pieces.

Puff Pastry Straws

ingredients

1 package frozen puff pastry, thawed

4 tablespoons (½ stick) butter, melted

1 tablespoon honey Dijon mustard

1 cup (4 ounces) grated Gruyère
   or cheese of your choice

1 egg white, lightly beaten

directions

Preheat the oven to 400 degrees. Grease a baking sheet.

Unfold the pastry sheet. Brush with melted butter, then with the mustard. Spread the cheese over the pastry, leaving a ½-inch border along the short edges. Press the cheese into the pastry, and cut the pastry into strips lengthwise. Twist each strip and place on the prepared baking sheet. Brush each strip with egg white. Bake for 15 minutes.

Note: For delicious variations on these puff pastry straws, try a topping of goat cheese, green onion and figs, or a sun-dried tomato, basil and feta topping. Press the mixture into the softened pastry, then cut into strips and twist. It's a little messy, but guests will appreciate the extra effort.

Makes about 15 pieces

Pimento Cheese

ingredients

1 (4-ounce) jar pimentos, drained

4 ounces medium Cheddar
cheese, shredded

4 ounces Colby Jack cheese, shredded

¼ to ½ teaspoon hot red pepper sauce

¼ cup mayonnaise

¼ cup cream cheese, at room temperature

Salt and cayenne pepper to taste

½ cup minced green onions,
additional Cheddar cheese
and minced garlic (optional)

directions

Combine the pimentos, Cheddar cheese and Colby Jack cheese in a food processor and pulse to combine. Transfer to a large bowl. Add the hot sauce and mayonnaise and mix well. In a separate bowl, whip the cream cheese until fluffy. Add to the Cheddar cheese mixture and mix well. Season with salt and cayenne pepper to taste. Add any optional ingredients and mix well. Serve right away or refrigerate.

Makes about 2 cups.

Cheesy Crab Dip

ingredients

8 ounces cream cheese, softened

½ cup mayonnaise

½ cup (2 ounces) shredded Monterey Jack cheese

½ cup (2 ounces) shredded or grated Parmesan cheese

1½ teaspoons Worcestershire sauce

½ cup marinated artichoke hearts, drained and roughly chopped

4 green onions, chopped, divided

Dash of hot sauce (optional)

8 ounces crabmeat

Additional Parmesan for topping (optional)

Pita chips, crackers or tortilla chips for serving

directions

Preheat the oven to 350 degrees. Combine the cream cheese, mayonnaise, Monterey Jack cheese, Parmesan cheese, Worcestershire sauce, artichoke hearts, half of the green onions and the hot sauce in a bowl and mix well. Fold in the crabmeat gently. Spoon into an 8-inch square baking dish. Top with additional Parmesan if desired. Bake for 30 minutes until hot and bubbly and beginning to brown on top. Sprinkle with the remaining green onions. Serve with pita chips, crackers or tortilla chips.

Note: This dip can be served as a passed appetizer by spooning the uncooked mixture onto rounds cut from thinly sliced white bread. Arrange them on a baking sheet and sprinkle with a little cayenne pepper. Bake at 350 degrees for about 15 minutes until the mixture begins to bubble and brown. These rounds can be assembled ahead of time, covered and refrigerated or frozen for later use.

Makes about 3 cups.

Shrimp Dip

ingredients

8 ounces cream cheese,
   at room temperature

½ cup mayonnaise

2 tablespoons ketchup or chili sauce

1 teaspoon Worcestershire sauce

¼ teaspoon garlic powder

½ pound head-off shrimp, boiled,
   peeled, deveined and diced

⅓ cup finely diced onion

Salt and black pepper to taste

Endive leaves or crackers for serving

directions

Combine the cream cheese, mayonnaise, ketchup, Worcestershire sauce and garlic powder in a medium bowl with a hand mixer until creamy. Stir in the shrimp and onion. Season with salt and pepper to taste. Serve on endive leaves or with crackers.

Makes 2 cups.

Hot Southwest Spinach Dip

ingredients

1 (10-ounce) package frozen chopped
   spinach, thawed and squeezed dry

8 ounces cream cheese, softened

½ cup salsa

1½ teaspoons ground cumin

2 cups (8 ounces) Mexican-blend
   shredded cheese

Tortilla chips for serving

directions

Preheat the oven to 350 degrees

Combine the spinach, cream cheese, salsa and cumin in a saucepan. Heat, stirring, until the mixture is hot and well blended. Pour into a 10-inch pie pan or quiche dish. Top with Mexican-blend cheese. Bake for 20 minutes, or until the cheese is bubbly. Serve with tortilla chips.

Makes 12 servings.

Cucumber Dip

ingredients

2 large cucumbers, peeled and seeded

½ cup apple cider vinegar

2 teaspoons salt

½ teaspoon garlic powder

8 ounces cream cheese

½ to ¾ cup mayonnaise

Salt to taste

Wheat crackers or vegetable crackers
    for serving

directions

Grate the cucumbers on the medium blade of a grater or food processor. Combine with the vinegar and 2 teaspoons salt in a bowl. Cover and refrigerate for at least 8 hours.

Drain the cucumbers, reserving the liquid. Squeeze the shredded cucumbers in a paper towel or clean kitchen towel to press out excess liquid. Combine the garlic powder, cream cheese and mayonnaise in a bowl with a hand mixer until well blended. Fold in the cucumbers by hand, adding reserved liquid as needed to thin to a dip consistency. Season with salt to taste. Serve with wheat crackers or vegetable crackers.

Makes 3 to 4 cups.

cucumber sandwiches

This dip can be made into delicious cucumber sandwiches. Remove crusts from one loaf of thinly sliced white bread and lightly butter the slices. Stir ¼ to ½ teaspoon horseradish into cucumber dip. Spread between two slices of bread. Cut each sandwich into 8 pieces. Can be made ahead, covered, and refrigerated for up to 2 days before serving.

Endive Spears with Pears

ingredients

3 tablespoons butter

2 tablespoons sugar

2 pears, peeled and diced

2 garlic cloves, chopped

1 tablespoon red wine vinegar

1 teaspoon salt

1 teaspoon black pepper

¼ cup extra-virgin olive oil

½ cup crumbled Stilton cheese

25 endive spears

½ cup pecan halves, toasted and chopped

directions

Melt the butter with the sugar in a pan over medium heat. Add the pears and cook until caramelized.

Whisk the garlic, vinegar, salt, pepper and olive oil in a bowl. Add the Stilton.

Spoon the cheese mixture into the endive spears. Top with the pears and pecans.

Note: This recipe doubles well. The pear mixture, Stilton and pecans are also delicious served over sturdy greens as a composed salad.

Makes 25 pieces.

Bar-B-Cue Cups

ingredients

¾ pound ground beef

¼ teaspoon salt

½ teaspoon black pepper

2 tablespoons minced Vidalia onion

½ cup barbecue sauce

1 tablespoon brown sugar

1 (8-ounce) can refrigerated biscuits

¾ cup (3 ounces) shredded
   Cheddar cheese

2 green onions, chopped

directions

Preheat the oven to 400 degrees.

Season the ground beef with salt and pepper. Sauté with the Vidalia onion in a large skillet; drain well. Add the barbecue sauce and brown sugar and mix well. Check for seasoning and add salt and pepper to taste.

Separate the biscuit dough into 12 equal pieces. Press each piece into an ungreased, regular-sized muffin cup, press the dough up the side to the edge of the cup. Spoon a heaping tablespoon of the meat mixture into each dough cup. Sprinkle with the cheese. Bake for 12 to 15 minutes, or until the biscuits are brown. Top with green onions.

Makes 12 servings.

Black Bean Hummus

ingredients

2 (15-ounce) cans black beans

¾ cup chopped roasted red pepper, from a jar or homemade

¼ cup lime juice

½ bunch green onions, coarsely chopped

4 garlic cloves, chopped, or 2 teaspoons garlic powder

3 tablespoons olive oil (omit if using jarred roasted red peppers in oil)

1½ teaspoons ground chipotle pepper

1½ teaspoons ground cumin

¼ teaspoon cayenne pepper

Salt, cayenne pepper, olive oil and lime juice to taste

Tortilla chips or pita chips for serving

directions

Drain the beans through a strainer, reserving the liquid. Combine the beans, red pepper, lime juice, green onions, garlic, olive oil, chipotle pepper, cumin and cayenne pepper in a food processor. Pulse a few times, then stir down, scraping the side. Add half the black bean liquid and process until the mixture begins to come together. Add more black bean liquid and/or olive oil to achieve the desired consistency. Taste and adjust the seasoning with salt, cayenne pepper and lime juice. Serve with tortilla chips or pita chips.

Note: Leftovers are great in chopped salads, burritos, enchiladas or quesadillas. You can substitute a fresh bell pepper for the roasted pepper, and ¼ of a small onion, diced, for the green onions for a distinctly fresh, bright flavor.

Makes about 2 cups.

our beginning

The Georgia Historical Society states that, "The International Order of the King's Daughters and Sons began on January 13, 1886 in New York City. Its purpose was the development of spiritual life and the stimulation of Christian activities. Margaret Bottome was the order's first president, serving until her death in 1906. The Georgia Branch did charity work with the incurably ill." In 1925, two circles of The King's Daughters—The Margaret Bottome Circle and The Elizabeth Butler Circle—joined volunteer forces to become a Junior Service League. On January 7, 1926, this organization was admitted to membership in The Association of Junior Leagues of America, and is now known as the Junior League of Savannah, serving the greater Savannah area, Hilton Head Island and Lowcountry, and Brunswick and the Golden Isles.

Slow Cooker Boiled Peanuts

ingredients

⅓ cup salt

2 cups warm water, plus enough to fill slow cooker

2 pounds green/raw peanuts

directions

Stir the salt into the water in a slow cooker until the salt dissolves. Rinse peanuts in a colander and add them to the slow cooker. Add water to within an inch of the top of the cooker. Cover and cook 8 hours or overnight on low, or 5 hours on high, or until desired tenderness is achieved. Stir every two hours (if not cooking overnight). Allow peanuts to stand in hot liquid and cool slightly before handling. For those who enjoy spice, boil peanuts with a bag of Zatarain's crab boil.

Makes 2 pounds of peanuts.

Boiled Peanut Hummus

ingredients

1 cup shelled boiled peanuts

1 tablespoon chopped fresh parsley

2 tablespoons fresh lemon juice

2 tablespoons peanut butter

1½ teaspoons hot red pepper sauce

2 garlic cloves, minced

½ teaspoon ground cumin

2 tablespoons olive oil

Water as needed

Salt and cayenne pepper to taste

Pretzel chips, crackers and raw vegetables for serving

directions

Combine the peanuts, parsley, lemon juice, peanut butter, hot sauce, garlic and cumin in a food processor. Process until coarsely chopped. Scrape down the side of the bowl. With the motor running, slowly add the olive oil in a thin stream, processing until smooth. Stir in up to 5 tablespoons water, 1 tablespoon at a time, to achieve the desired consistency. Season to taste with salt and cayenne pepper.

Note: During the summer, be sure to freeze some shelled peanuts to make this delicious dip during tailgate and oyster roast season. Support those Georgia peanut farmers!

Makes about 1 cup.

Southern Dill Pickle Deviled Eggs

ingredients

8 hard-boiled large eggs

2 tablespoons minced dill pickle or drained dill relish (Claussen's preferred)

¼ cup mayonnaise

1 tablespoon spicy mustard

1 tablespoon honey Dijon mustard or honey mustard

Salt and black pepper to taste

Paprika for garnish

directions

Cut the eggs into halves lengthwise. Scoop the yolks into a bowl. Add the pickle, mayonnaise and mustards. Beat with a hand mixer for a stiffer texture, or mash with a fork for a creamier texture. Taste the mixture and season with salt and pepper. Spoon the yolk mixture into a pastry bag or ziptop bag with a corner cut off. Fill the egg whites with the yolk mixture. Sprinkle with paprika for color and flavor.

Makes 16 servings.

the perfect hard-boiled egg

Place eggs in a saucepan large enough to hold them in a single layer. Add cold water to cover eggs by 1 inch. Set over high heat and bring the water to a rolling boil. Remove saucepan from heat and cover. Let eggs stand in the hot water for 12 minutes for large eggs for a firm, hard-boiled egg.

Fill a bowl with ice water. Remove cooked eggs from saucepan with a slotted spoon and tap each gently on the countertop. Transfer the eggs to the bowl and let stand for at least 1 minute. Refrigerate if not using immediately. When ready to use, peel and enjoy!

Pigs in a Blanket

ingredients

½ recipe Butter Horn Rolls (page 50)

¼ to ⅓ cup Dijon or Creole mustard

24 cocktail franks

directions

Preheat the oven to 375 degrees.

Roll and cut the dough as directed in the Butter Horn Roll recipe. Brush each triangle with some mustard. Place a cocktail frank about one-third from the bottom of each triangle. Roll to enclose. Place on a baking sheet. Bake for 12 to 15 minutes, or until lightly browned.

Makes 24 pieces.

Sausage Balls

The sausage mixture also makes delicious meatballs for a main dish.

ingredients

5 green onions, minced

2 garlic cloves, minced

2 pounds bulk Italian sausage
   (a combination of both hot and mild),
   or links with casings removed

1 egg, beaten

½ cup Italian bread crumbs

Salt, black pepper and cayenne
   pepper to taste

¼ cup (1 ounce) grated Parmesan cheese

1 (8-ounce) jar hot pepper jelly

directions

Preheat the oven to 400 degrees.

Combine the green onions, garlic and sausage in a bowl and mix well. Add the egg, bread crumbs, salt, black pepper and cayenne pepper and mix well. Roll the mixture into 1-inch balls. Arrange on a rimmed baking sheet and bake for 20 minutes or until browned, stirring frequently.

When ready to serve, heat the pepper jelly in the microwave, adding a tablespoon or two of water to thin to dipping consistency. Serve the sausage balls on wooden picks with melted hot pepper jelly for dipping.

Note: After the sausage mixture is shaped into balls, they can be frozen. Defrost before baking.

Makes 15 to 20 servings.

Black-Eyed Pea-co de Gallo

ingredients

½ onion, finely chopped

1 green bell pepper, chopped

1 bunch green onions, chopped

2 jalapeño peppers,
  seeded and minced

4 garlic cloves, minced

1 pint grape tomatoes, cut into quarters

¼ cup red wine vinegar

¼ cup vegetable oil

1 teaspoon salt

½ teaspoon black pepper

¼ teaspoon dried thyme

½ teaspoon prepared mustard

2 (15-ounce) cans black-eyed
  peas, drained

1 bunch cilantro, chopped

Tortilla chips for serving

directions

Stir together the onion, bell pepper, green onions, jalapeños, garlic, tomatoes, vinegar, oil, salt, pepper, thyme, mustard and black-eyed peas in a large bowl. Refrigerate to chill. When ready to serve, add the cilantro and mix well. Serve with tortilla chips.

Makes about 8 cups.

Photo courtesy of the Georgia Historical Society

Wartime efforts by the Junior League of Savannah included medical care. League member Mrs. Robert Hitch served as the League's volunteer chairman of the Red Cross Home Service and is shown here in her volunteer uniform in 1942.

SALADS & SOUPS

WRIGHT SQUARE, PERCIVAL WARD — 1733

The second most important of Savannah's squares, Wright Square, was first known as Upper Square and later Court House Square, after Oglethorpe's 1736 order to erect a courthouse. Every man, whether witness or defendant, pleaded his own case, since lawyers were originally banned from the colony. The 1889 Chatham County Courthouse still presides over Wright Square.

As the colony grew, so did the square's importance. The square was renamed Percival after its ward's namesake, John Lord Viscount Percival, Earl of Egmont and the first president of the Georgia Trustees.

Percival Square was the site of Georgia's first funeral procession for native son Tomo-chi-chi, "Mico" (chief) of the Yamacraw Indians, who befriended and guided Oglethorpe and protected the colonists by negotiating peace with the Uchee, Lower Creek, and other surrounding Georgia Indian tribes. After his death, at his request, Tomo-chi-chi's body was transported by canoe to the heart of the city, Percival Square. As esteemed in death as in life, Mico's body was interred in the square. Oglethorpe ordered a pyramid of stone erected over the grave as an ornament to the city and a testimony of gratitude.

When Georgia became a royal colony, the square's name was changed to Wright Square, in honor of Sir James Wright, Georgia's third and last royal governor. Wright's appointment was celebrated in 1762 with Savannah's first public ball, described as "the most numerous and brilliant appearance ever known in the town." Under Wright's rule, peace, growth, and prosperity flourished.

Savannah's newspapers report that when "…the ward's tithings were partitioned, the extreme portion of the square was cut. It was on this portion (133 York Street) that the remains of Tomo-chi-chi and his coffin were discovered on February 15, 1878." In 1883, the Central of Georgia Railroad constructed a monument to its founder, William Washington Gordon, in the center of the square. In the southwest corner, Gordon's daughter-in-law, Nellie Gordon, ordered a new monument be made in Tomo-chi-chi's memory, a large granite boulder installed on April 21, 1899. The Georgia Society of Colonial Dames dedicated it as a permanent monument to the friendship, loyalty, and deeds of Tomo-chi-chi.

opposite page: A century old live oak canopy shades Wright Square.

Grilled Corn and Tomato Summer Salad

ingredients

4 ears corn (yellow, white or a mix), shucked and silks removed

2 cups cherry tomatoes, sliced

¼ cup fresh basil, sliced in chiffonade

2 tablespoons chopped fresh chives

Juice of 1½ limes

2 to 3 tablespoons extra-virgin olive oil

Baby salad greens, such as arugula or watercress

Chopped avocado, crumbled bacon or feta cheese for garnish (optional)

directions

In large stockpot of water, boil the corn for 7 minutes. Transfer to a grill and grill the corn until thoroughly cooked and slightly charred. Combine the tomatoes, basil, chives, lime juice, olive oil and salad greens in a bowl and mix well. Cut the corn from the cobs and add to the bowl. Toss to combine. Season to taste with salt and black pepper, and garnish with avocado, bacon or feta cheese, if desired.

Note: Grilling the corn is a must for this quintessential summer salad—a perfect accompaniment to everything from burgers to pork tenderloin.

Makes 4 to 6 servings.

Tomatoes with Parsley and Parmesan Cheese

ingredients

2 garlic cloves, minced

½ cup extra-virgin olive oil

3 tablespoons red wine vinegar

1 cup packed fresh parsley (preferably curly), coarsely chopped

4 medium tomatoes, chopped

Salt and black pepper to taste

½ cup (2 ounces) freshly grated Parmesan cheese

directions

Combine the garlic, olive oil and vinegar in a bowl and whisk to blend. Pour over the parsley and tomatoes in a bowl and toss to coat. Season to taste with salt and pepper. Add the Parmesan just before serving, mixing well.

Makes 4 to 6 servings.

Mandarin Orange and Candied Pecan Spinach Salad

ingredients

CANDIED PECANS

1 cup sugar

¼ cup cinnamon (or to taste)

2 teaspoons salt

2 egg whites

10 drops vanilla extract

1 pound pecans

SWEET-SOUR-SPICY DRESSING

⅔ cup vegetable or other mild-flavored oil

⅓ cup cider vinegar

1 tablespoon sugar

2 tablespoons chopped fresh parsley

1 teaspoon salt

¼ teaspoon black pepper

¼ teaspoon red pepper flakes

SALAD

3 ounces mixed greens

3 ounces baby spinach

Very thinly sliced red onion

1 hard-boiled egg, sliced

1 (11-ounce) can mandarin oranges

directions

For the candied pecans, preheat the oven to 350 degrees. Combine the sugar, cinnamon and salt in a bowl and set aside. Combine the egg whites and vanilla in a bowl and mix well. Add 10 to 15 pecans at a time to the egg whites, stirring to coat, and then add the pecans to the sugar mixture and toss to coat. Arrange the pecans, not touching, on a nonstick baking sheet. Bake for 10 minutes. Let cool until firm, and then remove from the baking sheet.

For the dressing, combine all ingredients in a bowl with a whisk or shake to blend in a jar with a tight-fitting lid.

For the salad, combine the greens and spinach. Divide among four salad plates. Top each with several slices of red onion. Divide the egg and mandarin oranges among the plates. Drizzle with a bit of the dressing. Top with pecans.

Makes 4 servings.

Jackson Salad

ingredients

1 (14-ounce) can artichoke hearts, drained and chopped

1 (14-ounce) can hearts of palm, drained and chopped

2 tablespoons chopped parsley

½ cup chopped cooked bacon

2 garlic cloves, pressed

4 ounces blue cheese, crumbled

2 tablespoons lemon juice

⅓ cup vegetable oil

Salt and black pepper to taste

1 package romaine lettuce hearts, chopped

directions

Combine the artichoke hearts, hearts of palm, parsley, bacon, garlic, blue cheese, lemon juice, oil, salt and pepper in a large bowl and mix well. Refrigerate until ready to use. Just before serving, add the lettuce and toss to combine.

Makes 4 servings.

Honey Chicken Salad

ingredients

4 cups chopped cooked chicken

3 celery ribs, chopped (about 1½ cups)

1 cup dried cranberries

½ cup chopped toasted pecans

1 cup mayonnaise

½ cup plain yogurt, drained

⅓ cup orange blossom honey

¼ teaspoon salt

¼ teaspoon black pepper

1 tablespoon poppy seeds

directions

Combine the chicken, celery, cranberries and pecans in a bowl and toss to mix. Whisk the mayonnaise, yogurt, honey, salt and pepper in a separate bowl. Add to the chicken mixture and stir gently to blend. Add the poppy seeds and toss lightly.

Makes 4 luncheon servings.

Succotash Salad

ingredients

1 pound shelled fresh or frozen butterbeans

Salt to taste

2½ cups fresh corn, cooked (cut from about 5 large ears)

⅓ cup chopped red onion

2 tablespoons chopped fresh thyme

1 (4-ounce) jar diced pimentos, drained

¼ cup lemon juice

3 tablespoons vegetable oil

¾ teaspoon salt

¼ teaspoon black pepper

White pepper to taste

Finely chopped green onions and cooked crumbled bacon for garnish

directions

Bring a pot of salted water to a boil over medium-high heat. Add the butterbeans and cook 2 minutes if using frozen, or simmer, covered, for 25 to 30 minutes until tender if using fresh. Drain in a colander and rinse with cold water.

Mix the butterbeans, corn, onion, thyme and pimentos in a bowl. In a small jar (such as the pimento jar) combine the lemon juice, oil, salt and black pepper. Shake vigorously to combine. Pour over the corn mixture and toss to combine. Let stand for at least 15 minutes, or cover and refrigerate for up to 2 days. Before serving, adjust the seasoning with salt and white pepper. Garnish with green onions and bacon.

Makes 4 to 6 servings.

Cauliflower Soup

ingredients

6 cups cauliflower florets and stems

5 cups chicken stock, divided

5 tablespoons butter

5 tablespoons all-purpose flour

3 cups half-and-half

1 to 1½ teaspoons white pepper

1½ teaspoons salt

directions

Cook the cauliflower in 3 cups of the stock in a large pot until tender. Process the cauliflower and stock with an immersion blender, or in a blender or food processor, until smooth. Heat the butter in a Dutch oven. Whisk in the flour until well blended. Whisk in the remaining stock and cook for 5 to 10 minutes until thickened. Add the half-and-half, cauliflower, white pepper and salt. Cook for 15 to 20 minutes to desired thickness. Adjust the seasonings and serve hot or cold.

Makes about 10 cups.

Mike Senior's Crab Stew

ingredients

16 tablespoons (2 sticks) butter

1 bell pepper, finely chopped

1 medium onion, finely chopped

½ cup all-purpose flour

2 quarts (8 cups) half-and-half

¾ teaspoon salt, or to taste

½ teaspoon black pepper

¼ teaspoon white pepper

1 (4-ounce) jar pimentos, drained, or ½ cup finely chopped red bell pepper

1 pound crabmeat (preferably lump, but claw meat will work), picked through for bits of shell

1 pint (2 cups) heavy whipping cream

1 teaspoon filé powder (optional)

1 tablespoon sherry, or to taste

directions

Melt 1 stick of the butter in a large pot and sauté the bell pepper and onion until tender. Whisk in the flour and cook, stirring constantly, until the roux smells nutty and is light brown. Add 1 quart of the half-and-half slowly, stirring continuously. Reduce the heat and simmer for 10 to 15 minutes, stirring occasionally. Do not boil. Season with salt, black pepper and white pepper. Add the pimentos. Adjust the consistency with additional half-and-half if needed. Add the crabmeat, heavy cream, and the remaining stick of butter, stirring just to blend. Stir in the file powder and remaining half-and-half (use less, if desired). Heat over a low simmer without boiling to serving temperature. Finish with sherry and serve immediately.

Note: The soup can be made ahead and refrigerated. A lighter stew can be made by substituting 1 quart seafood stock for 2 quarts half and half and omitting the final stick of butter. Bring to a simmer after the addition of crabmeat and heavy cream, let cook briefly, and adjust thickness with additional stock if needed.

Makes 8 to 10 servings.

Texas Tortilla Soup

ingredients

2 to 4 tablespoons butter

¼ cup vegetable oil

1 large onion, chopped

1 jalapeño pepper, seeded and chopped

4 garlic cloves, minced

6 ribs celery, diced

1 teaspoon ground cumin

1 teaspoon chili powder

1 teaspoon salt

1 teaspoon lemon pepper seasoning

3 teaspoons hot red pepper sauce

½ cup all-purpose flour

1 rotisserie chicken, meat shredded

2 (14-ounce) cans tomatoes

1 (15-ounce) can black beans

1 (16-ounce) can sweet corn

5 cups chicken broth or homemade stock
    (see page 101)

8 corn tortillas, cut into strips

Sour cream, sliced avocado and shredded
    Cheddar cheese for garnish

directions

Heat the butter and oil in a stockpot (preferably nonstick) over medium-high heat. Add the onion, jalapeño, garlic and celery and sauté for 5 minutes. Stir in the cumin, chili powder, salt, lemon pepper, hot sauce and flour and mix well. Add the chicken, tomatoes, beans, corn and broth and mix well. Reduce the heat to low and simmer for 1 hour.

Preheat the oven to 375 degrees. Cover a baking sheet with foil and spray with nonstick cooking spray. Arrange the tortilla strips on the baking sheet and spray with nonstick cooking spray. Bake for 10 to 15 minutes until the strips are toasted and beginning to brown on the edges.

To serve, divide the tortilla strips among 6 to 8 bowls, reserving some for garnish. Fill the bowls with soup. Top each bowl with a spoonful each of sour cream, avocado, cheese and remaining tortilla strips.

Makes 6 to 8 servings.

Steak Chili

Serve this spicy chili with cornbread.

ingredients

5 pounds sirloin steak,
   cut into 1-inch cubes

¼ cup vegetable oil

5 onions, chopped

6 garlic cloves, minced

2 to 4 jalapeño peppers,
   seeded and chopped

2 to 4 serrano chiles, seeded and chopped

¼ cup chili powder (up to 2 tablespoons
   can be ancho chile powder; up
   to 1 tablespoon can be chipotle
   chile powder)

2 tablespoons ground cumin

1 teaspoon cayenne pepper

1½ teaspoons salt

1 teaspoon black pepper

¼ teaspoon red pepper flakes

2 (15-ounce) cans fire-roasted tomatoes

2 (15-ounce) cans kidney beans

Green onions, sour cream, shredded
   Cheddar cheese for serving

directions

Brown the steak in the oil in a large pot. Add the onions, garlic, jalapeños and serranos and cook until the onions are translucent. Add the chili powder, cumin, cayenne pepper, salt, black pepper, red pepper flakes, tomatoes and beans and mix well. Simmer, covered, for 1 hour. Remove the cover and stir, scraping the bottom. Simmer, uncovered, for 30 to 45 minutes. Serve with green onions, sour cream and Cheddar cheese.

Makes 12 to 15 servings.

Sicilian Sausage Soup

Part pasta, part soup, this is an Italian twist on delicious, cold weather comfort food. It's a full meal by itself and wonderful served with crusty garlic bread.

ingredients

1 pound bulk Italian sausage, mild or sweet

1 large onion, chopped

½ cup chopped carrots

½ cup chopped celery

2 garlic cloves, minced

2 tablespoons olive oil

1 (10-ounce) can tomato soup

2 teaspoons dried oregano

1 teaspoon dried rosemary

2 teaspoons dried basil

½ teaspoon black pepper

1 teaspoon fennel seeds

2 (16-ounce) cans diced
   tomatoes, undrained

8 cups chicken broth or homemade stock
   (see page 101)

½ cup orzo

Chopped black or Kalamata olives and
   Parmesan cheese for garnish (optional)

directions

Brown the sausage in a stockpot, stirring to break it up. When cooked through, drain and discard the grease. Remove the sausage from the pot and set aside. In the same stockpot, sauté the onion, carrots, celery and garlic in the olive oil until tender. Add the cooked sausage, tomato soup, oregano, rosemary, basil, black pepper, fennel seeds, tomatoes and broth. Cover, bring to a boil, and then reduce the heat to simmer. Cook for 1 hour, stirring occasionally. Stir in the orzo and cook for 30 minutes, stirring frequently. Serve garnished with olives and Parmesan cheese.

Makes 6 servings.

BREADS

CHIPPEWA SQUARE, BROWN WARD — 1815

Savannah's close proximity to the British Atlantic blockade, warships, and privateers necessitated a constant state of readiness during the War of 1812. When America's second victory of independence was declared on February 28, 1815, euphoria spread and U.S. nationalism heightened.

Both Brown Ward and Chippewa Square were named to commemorate Major-General Jacob Brown (1775-1828), an American hero in the War of 1812 and commanding general of the U.S. Army forces that won the Battle of Chippewa. Chippewa Square is distinguished by a 1910 bronze monument erected to commemorate Georgia's founder, James Edward Oglethorpe. The life-size statue is the work of sculptor Daniel Chester French, and its base was designed by Henry Bacon; both were artists for the Lincoln Memorial in Washington D.C. Chippewa Square quickly became the center for theater and musical productions held at the 1818 Savannah Theater. However, Savannah's theatrical nightlife was kept in check by the adjacent First Baptist and Independent Presbyterian Churches, as well as the Chatham Academy, predecessor of the Savannah-Chatham County public schools and the center of education in Savannah.

The great wave of nationalist feeling that followed the War of 1812 led to a period of economic prosperity in Savannah that lasted until the outbreak of the Civil War. An awakened cultural consciousness spawned great interest in the fine arts, including poetry, oratory, painting, sculpture, and architecture.

Savannah's fortunes were invested in its public buildings and also in elaborate private dwellings that became centers of social and cultural activities.

Photo courtesy of the Georgia Historical Society

An ongoing emphasis throughout the Junior League of Savannah's history continues today with a focus on care for the most vulnerable, especially the poorest children and the elderly. Volunteer Mrs. Charles Drayton cares for children in 1942.

opposite page: Sword drawn, James Edward Oglethorpe continues to watch over Savannah from Chippewa Square.

Butter Horn Rolls

ingredients

1 cup milk

10 ounces (2½ sticks) butter

½ cup sugar

1 teaspoon salt

1 package dry yeast

2 eggs

4 cups all-purpose flour

directions

Heat the milk, butter, sugar and salt in a saucepan until bubbles form around the edge. Cool to lukewarm. Pour the mixture into the bowl of a mixer. Add the yeast and let stand for 5 minutes until dissolved. Add the eggs and beat to combine. Add the flour 2 cups at a time, beating well after each addition. Cover and refrigerate the dough for at least 6 hours.

Lightly dust a clean surface with flour and roll the dough to ¼-inch thickness. Cut into long triangles. Roll each triangle from the wide end. Arrange on a greased baking sheet. Set in a warm place to rise for 2½ hours, or until doubled in size.

Preheat the oven to 375 degrees. Bake the rolls for 12 to 15 minutes, or until golden brown.

Makes 30 to 35 rolls.

Sour Cream Rolls

ingredients

2 cups self-rising flour

12 tablespoons (1½ sticks)
   butter, softened

8 ounces sour cream

directions

Preheat the oven to 350 degrees. Grease mini muffin cups. Mix the flour and butter in a blender until well combined. Add the sour cream and mix well. Spoon the batter into the muffin cups. Bake for 20 to 25 minutes, or until light brown.

Note: This versatile dough takes well to additions like cheese, herbs, garlic or green onions.

Makes about 36 rolls.

Angel Biscuits

ingredients

1 package yeast

2½ cups sifted self-rising flour

2 tablespoons plus 2 teaspoons sugar

½ teaspoon baking soda

½ cup shortening

1 cup buttermilk, at room temperature

directions

Dissolve the yeast in 2 tablespoons warm water. Sift the flour, sugar and baking soda together into a bowl. Add the shortening and buttermilk. Add the yeast mixture. Mix lightly with a fork, then knead by hand 3 or 4 times until just combined. Do not overmix.

Sprinkle self-rising flour over a work surface. Roll the dough to a 1 inch thickness. Cut with a biscuit cutter. Arrange the biscuits on a baking sheet. Let rise for 1 to 2 hours.

Preheat the oven to 425 degrees. Bake the biscuits for 10 to 12 minutes, or until golden brown..

Note: The dough can be stored in the refrigerator for up to 2 weeks. This recipe doubles well.

Makes 12 biscuits.

Cinnamon Sugar–Crusted Popovers or Muffins

ingredients

1 cup 2% or whole milk

2 tablespoons unsalted butter, melted

2 jumbo or 3 large eggs

1 teaspoon vanilla extract

1 teaspoon almond extract

½ teaspoon salt

1½ tablespoons sugar

1 cup all-purpose flour

CINNAMON-SUGAR TOPPING

1 tablespoon cinnamon

1 cup sugar

2 tablespoons butter, melted

directions

Preheat the oven to 400 degrees. Grease a popover or muffin pan.

Combine the milk, butter, eggs, vanilla extract, almond extract, salt, sugar and flour in a blender or with an immersion blender. Blend for 10 seconds, or until well combined.

Fill each muffin cup half to two-thirds full, dividing the batter evenly. Bake for 35 minutes or until golden brown. Let cool 3 minutes in the pan. Remove to a wire rack.

For the cinnamon-sugar topping, combine the cinnamon and sugar in a medium container with a lid. (The container should be large enough to hold a single popover.) Shake to combine. As soon as the popovers are cool enough to handle, brush one with butter, and then put it into the container with the cinnamon sugar. Shake to coat. Repeat with the remaining popovers.

Makes 6 popovers or 9 muffins.

Cinnamon Rolls

ingredients

DOUGH

2½ to 2¾ cups all-purpose flour, divided

3 tablespoons sugar

1 teaspoon salt

2¼ teaspoons yeast

½ cup water

¼ cup milk

2½ tablespoons butter

1 egg

FILLING

4 tablespoons (½ stick) butter, softened

⅓ cup sugar

2 tablespoons cinnamon

GLAZE

1½ cups confectioners' sugar

¼ cup milk or brewed coffee

1½ teaspoons vanilla extract,
   or 1 tablespoons maple syrup

directions

For the dough, combine 2¼ cups of the flour, the sugar, salt and yeast in a bowl. Heat the water, milk and butter in a saucepan to 115 to 120 degrees, about the temperature of hot bath water. Pour into the flour mixture and mix just until combined. Add the egg and ¼ to ½ cup of flour to make a soft dough. Knead on a floured surface for 3 to 4 minutes. Return the dough to a greased bowl and let rest for 10 minutes.

For the filling, roll the dough into a 14 x 8-inch rectangle. Spread with the softened butter. Sprinkle with the sugar and cinnamon. Roll from the long edge to enclose the filling. Cut into approximately 12 rolls.

Arrange the rolls in a greased 9-inch square baking dish. Let rise in a warm place for 60 to 90 minutes until doubled in size. Preheat the oven to 375 degrees. Bake for 25 to 30 minutes, covering with foil about halfway through baking to avoid over browning.

For the glaze, combine the confectioners' sugar, milk and vanilla in a small bowl. Blend until smooth. Drizzle over the hot rolls.

Makes 12 rolls.

Poppyseed Muffins

ingredients

3 eggs

2½ cups sugar

1¼ cups vegetable oil

1½ cups milk

1½ teaspoons salt

1½ teaspoons baking powder

2 tablespoons poppy seeds

1½ teaspoons vanilla extract

1½ teaspoons almond extract

3 cups all-purpose flour

directions

Preheat the oven to 350 degrees. Grease or line muffin cups in a standard sized tin.

Beat the eggs, sugar and oil in a bowl until well blended. Add the milk, salt, baking powder, poppy seeds, vanilla extract and almond extract. Mix just until blended. Add the flour, 1 cup at a time, until just combined. Do not overmix.

Fill muffin cups nearly to the top. Bake for 20 to 25 minutes.

Makes 24 to 36 muffins.

Nita's Pumpkin Bread

ingredients

1 teaspoon nutmeg

1 teaspoon cinnamon

3 cups sugar

1 cup vegetable oil

4 eggs

1½ teaspoons salt

1 cup canned pumpkin

⅔ cup water

2 teaspoons baking soda

1 cup chopped pecans

3 cups all-purpose flour

directions

Preheat the oven to 350 degrees. Coat three 8- or 9-inch loaf pans with nonstick cooking spray.

Combine the nutmeg, cinnamon, sugar, oil, eggs and salt in a large bowl and beat to combine. Add the pumpkin, water, soda, pecans and flour and mix well. Spoon the batter into the prepared pans. Bake for 55 to 60 minutes or until a wooden pick inserted in the center comes out clean.

Note: This bread can be frozen after baking.

Makes 3 loaves.

Zucchini Bread

ingredients

3 eggs

2 cups sugar

¾ cup vegetable oil

2 cups grated zucchini

1 tablespoon vanilla extract

3 cups all-purpose flour

1 teaspoon baking soda

1 teaspoon salt

1 teaspoon cinnamon

¼ teaspoon baking powder

½ cup dried cranberries, raisins or chopped nuts

directions

Preheat the oven to 325 degrees. Grease and flour two 9-inch loaf pans.

Beat the eggs in a large bowl with an electric mixer. Add the sugar, oil, zucchini and vanilla and mix well. Combine the flour, baking soda, salt, cinnamon and baking powder in another bowl. Sift into the egg mixture. Add the dried cranberries and mix well. Divide the batter evenly between the loaf pans. Bake for 60 to 80 minutes. The bread is done when a wooden pick inserted in the center of the loaf comes out clean.

Makes 2 loaves.

VEGETABLES & SIDES

MADISON SQUARE, JASPER WARD — 1837

In declaration of Savannah's revolutionary and nationalistic spirit, Madison Square and Jasper Ward were established in 1837. Madison Square was named for President James Madison, Jr., known as "Father of the Constitution." He was the author of the Bill of Rights, an American statesman, a political theorist, and a hero in Americans' hearts.

Centered in Madison Square is a bronze monument erected for Revolutionary War hero, Sergeant William Jasper. A three-day celebration attended by President Grover Cleveland followed the unveiling of the monument. Sgt. Jasper, a brilliant soldier, rescued shackled American prisoners at Jasper Springs and then placed the irons on British soldiers. Alexander Doyle's bronze monument depicts a heroic Jasper holding aloft his company's banner on the ramparts of Savannah, where he was mortally wounded. Jasper closed "his eyes upon the Revolution" at the Siege of Savannah in 1779, and lies among the brave dead somewhere beneath Savannah's soil.

The ward also played a role during the Civil War. It was here that General W.T. Sherman ended his "March to the Sea" by sparing Savannah and presenting the city to President Lincoln as a Christmas gift. Sherman's residence and headquarters were located in the Greene Mansion during the occupation of Savannah (1864-1865), and rent was collected, since Greene was a British citizen. It was here that Sherman's staff and local black community leaders conceived Sherman's Special Field

Orders No. 15, better known as "Forty Acres and a Mule," which settled freed slave refugees along the coastal Sea Islands.

Photo courtesy of the Georgia Historical Society

The League's first fund-raiser was the Junior League edition of the Savannah Morning News. Members also raised money by holding teas, balls, a horse show, and a golf tournament. The League held its first Follies in 1934.

opposite page: *Sergeant William Jasper holds the Standards high in Madison Square.*

Collard Greens

ingredients

- 1 bunch collard greens, ribs removed and leaves torn into bite-size pieces
- 2 tablespoons bacon drippings or vegetable oil
- 8 ounces ham or seasoning meat
- 1 onion, chopped
- 2 teaspoons finely chopped garlic
- ¼ teaspoon red pepper flakes
- 1 teaspoon salt
- 1 tablespoon Pickapepper sauce or red wine vinegar

directions

Rinse the greens in cold water several times to remove any grit.

Heat the bacon drippings in a large skillet. Add the ham and cook until browned. Add the onions and cook until translucent, stirring frequently. Add the garlic, pepper flakes, salt and greens. Cover and cook until the greens soften, turning occasionally.

Stir in the Pickapepper sauce and cook until the greens are tender. Remove the cover to cook off any excess liquid. Taste and adjust the seasonings as needed.

Makes 4 servings.

mexican collards

For a Mexican twist on collards, substitute chorizo for ham, and add 2 to 4 seeded and chopped poblano peppers with the onion.

Baked Eggplant and Tomatoes

ingredients

2 medium eggplant

Salt, black pepper and
cayenne pepper to taste

6 to 8 thin slices stale sourdough
or other crusty bread

1 garlic clove, peeled

2 tablespoons butter

1 large Vidalia onion, thinly sliced

3 pounds ripe tomatoes, thinly sliced

3 garlic cloves, minced

2 teaspoons fresh thyme, or ⅔ teaspoon
dried thyme

1 tablespoon fresh oregano, or 1 teaspoon
dried oregano

3 tablespoons sliced fresh basil

¼ teaspoon red pepper flakes

6 ounces fresh mozzarella, thinly sliced

directions

Slice the eggplant lengthwise into ½-inch planks. Salt lightly on both sides and drain on paper towels for 15 to 20 minutes. Season lightly with black pepper and cayenne pepper. Broil on high for 3 to 5 minutes per side.

Toast the bread lightly, then rub the whole garlic clove over the surface. Butter lightly and set aside.

Preheat the oven to 400 degrees. Layer the eggplant in an 8-inch square baking dish, cutting pieces so they fit together to cover the bottom completely. Scatter a handful of onion slices over the eggplant, then top with sliced tomatoes. Sprinkle with a third each of the garlic, thyme, oregano and basil plus a big pinch of red pepper flakes. Cover with a layer of mozzarella. Make a layer of toast, then continue layering eggplant, tomatoes, seasonings, mozzarella and toast. Omit the toast from the final layer. Alternate the direction of the eggplant layers for easier serving.

Bake until the cheese begins to brown.

Makes 6 servings.

Stuffed Sweet Peppers

ingredients

4 red, yellow, orange or green
   bell peppers

1 tablespoon extra-virgin olive oil

1 tablespoon balsamic vinegar

2 large garlic cloves, minced

Salt and freshly ground black pepper to taste

1 pound cherry tomatoes, cut into halves
   or quarters

1¼ cups cubed fresh mozzarella cheese

½ cup loosely packed fresh basil leaves,
   sliced into ribbons

directions

Preheat the oven to 375 degrees. Cut the peppers into halves lengthwise. Remove the seeds and ribs. Cut a thin slice from the rounded side of each half if needed to sit flat in a baking dish.

Whisk together the olive oil, vinegar, garlic, salt and pepper in a bowl. Add the tomatoes, mozzarella and basil and mix to coat. Fill each pepper with the stuffing mixture. Arrange the peppers in a baking dish. Bake, uncovered, for about 40 minutes until the peppers are tender.

Set the oven to broil. Broil the peppers for 1 minute or until the cheese is lightly browned.

Makes 8 servings.

Pesto-Topped Grilled Summer Squash

ingredients

½ cup pine nuts

½ cup chopped fresh basil

1 tablespoon extra-virgin olive oil

2 tablespoons grated Parmesan cheese

1 garlic clove, minced

2 teaspoons lemon juice

¼ teaspoon salt

2 medium summer squash (about 1
   pound), sliced diagonally ¼-inch thick

Canola or olive oil cooking spray

directions

Toast the pine nuts in a small nonstick skillet over medium heat until a light golden color, tossing as they begin to brown. Cool slightly, then finely chop.

Preheat a grill to medium-high. Combine the pine nuts, basil, olive oil, Parmesan, garlic, lemon juice and salt in a small bowl. Coat both sides of the squash slices with cooking spray. Grill for 2 to 3 minutes per side until browned and tender. Serve topped with pesto.

Makes 4 servings.

Fresh Tomato Pie

This fresh-tasting pie is best when made with homemade mayonnaise (page 166).

ingredients

2 or 3 large tomatoes, peeled and sliced

Salt to taste

1 (9-inch) unbaked pie shell

2 or 3 green onions, chopped

1 tablespoon chopped fresh basil

1 tablespoon chopped fresh chives

Black pepper to taste

1 cup mayonnaise, preferably homemade
    (page 166)

1 cup (4 ounces) shredded sharp
    Cheddar cheese

directions

Sprinkle the tomatoes lightly with salt. Set on a rack to drain for 15 to 20 minutes. Preheat the oven to 400 degrees.

Prick the bottom of the pie shell in several places. Bake for 12 to 15 minutes until the top edge is just beginning to brown. Remove from the oven and let cool completely.

Lower the oven temperature to 350 degrees. Layer the tomatoes, green onions, basil and chives in the cooled pie shell. Season with salt and pepper. Combine the mayonnaise and cheese in a mixing bowl. Spread over the tomato layer. Bake for 20 minutes, or until the top is lightly browned.

Makes 4 main-dish servings.

Okra and Tomatoes

Whether you use bacon drippings or oil is up to you—traditional and vegetarian versions of this dish are equally good.

ingredients

1 onion, chopped

1 pound okra, sliced

2 tablespoons bacon drippings
    or vegetable oil

3½ cups chopped tomatoes

1 teaspoon salt

2 garlic cloves, minced

1 bay leaf

1 sprig fresh thyme

directions

Sauté the onion and okra in the bacon drippings in a heavy skillet for about 3 minutes, stirring frequently until the okra is dry and no longer sticky. Add the tomatoes and remaining ingredients and mix well. Cover and simmer for 25 to 30 minutes.

Makes 4 servings..

Vidalia Onion Casserole

ingredients

5 Vidalia onions, sliced into rings

8 tablespoons (1 stick) butter

1 cup (4 ounces) grated Parmesan cheese

20 butter crackers, crushed

directions

Preheat the oven to 325 degrees.

Sauté the onions in the butter in a skillet until tender and translucent.

Layer half the onions in a 2-quart baking dish. Top with half of the cheese, and then half the crackers. Repeat with the remaining onions, cheese and crackers. Bake, uncovered, for 30 minutes.

Makes 6 to 8 servings.

Stovetop Macaroni and Cheese

ingredients

½ pound pasta (rotini and
   cavatappi hold sauce well)

Salt to taste

4 tablespoons (½ stick) butter

2 eggs

6 ounces evaporated milk,
   or a 5-ounce can evaporated milk plus
   1 ounce half-and-half or whole milk

½ teaspoon hot red pepper sauce,
   or to taste

1 teaspoon kosher salt

Freshly ground black pepper to taste

¾ teaspoon dry mustard

10 ounces Cheddar or a mixture of several
cheeses, shredded, plus more if desired

directions

Cook the pasta in a large pot of boiling salted water until al dente. Drain and return the pasta to the pot. Add the butter and toss to coat. Reduce the heat to low.

Whisk together the eggs, evaporated milk, hot sauce, kosher salt, pepper and mustard. Stir into the pasta and cook for 1 to 2 minutes until slightly thickened. Add the cheese and cook, stirring, for 2 to 3 minutes until the cheese is melted and the sauce is creamy. Add another handful of cheese, if needed. Serve immediately.

Makes 4 to 6 servings.

Spring Risotto

ingredients

½ pound fresh asparagus, preferably thin spears, trimmed and cut into 1½-inch sections

2 tablespoons olive oil

1 tablespoon butter

2 leeks, white and green parts chopped

2 garlic cloves, chopped

½ teaspoon kosher salt

¼ teaspoon black pepper

1 cup Arborio rice

1 cup dry white wine or dry sherry

3½ cups chicken stock, vegetable stock or water

1½ cups frozen peas, thawed

1 tablespoon lemon juice

½ cup (2 ounces) grated Parmesan cheese

1 teaspoon fresh oregano, chopped

1 teaspoon fresh thyme, chopped

2 teaspoons grated or finely chopped lemon zest

Grated Parmesan cheese and fresh thyme sprigs for garnish

directions

Heat the olive oil and butter in a large saucepan over medium heat. Add the leeks and cook, stirring occasionally, for 4 to 6 minutes until tender. Add the garlic, salt, pepper and rice and sauté for 2 minutes. Add the wine and cook until absorbed.

Add the stock to the rice mixture about ¾ cup at a time. Cook, stirring occasionally, until the rice absorbs the liquid before adding more. When half the stock has been used, add the asparagus. Continue adding stock by the ladleful until the rice is al dente but the consistency is still soupy, about 25 minutes. Stir in the peas and lemon juice. When the peas are warmed through, stir in the Parmesan, oregano, thyme and lemon zest. Adjust the seasoning or consistency if needed. Serve with additional Parmesan and fresh thyme sprigs for garnish.

Note: Trim an asparagus by holding a spear with an end in each hand, and then bend the stalk until it snaps at its natural point. You can add the tough ends of the stem to the stock for additional flavor.

Makes 2 main-course servings or 4 appetizer servings.

Zucchini Cornbread Casserole

ingredients

4 cups shredded zucchini

1 onion, chopped

2 eggs, beaten

1 (8-ounce) package corn muffin mix

½ teaspoon salt

¼ teaspoon black pepper

8 ounces Cheddar cheese, shredded

directions

Preheat the oven to 350 degrees. Grease a 2-quart baking dish.

Combine the zucchini, onion, eggs, muffin mix, salt and pepper. Stir in half of the cheese. Spread the mixture in the baking dish. Top with the remaining cheese. Bake for 1 hour.

Makes 6 to 8 servings.

Praline Sweet Potatoes

The member who contributed this recipe writes that it started as a Christmas dinner side dish rivalry between her mother and aunt, an annual showdown that lasted for years.

ingredients

SWEET POTATOES

3 cups mashed cooked sweet potatoes

1 cup granulated sugar

2 eggs

1 teaspoon vanilla extract

½ cup milk

8 tablespoons (1 stick) butter, melted

TOPPING

1 cup packed brown sugar

⅓ cup all-purpose flour

⅓ cup butter, melted

1 cup pecan pieces

directions

Preheat the oven to 350 degrees. Grease a 2-quart baking dish.

For the sweet potatoes, combine the sweet potatoes, sugar, eggs, vanilla, milk and butter in a bowl and mix well. Spoon into the baking dish.

For the topping, combine the brown sugar, flour, butter and pecans in a bowl and mix well. Spoon over the sweet potato mixture. Bake for 30 minutes.

Makes 8 servings.

Honey Lemon–Roasted Sweet Potatoes

ingredients

3 sweet potatoes

3 tablespoons olive oil

2 tablespoons honey

2 tablespoons lemon juice

Salt and black pepper to taste

directions

Preheat the oven to 400 degrees. Peel the sweet potatoes and cut into 1- to 2-inch cubes. Spread in a glass baking dish and drizzle with the olive oil, honey and lemon juice. Season lightly with salt and pepper. Toss to coat evenly.

Roast for 35 to 45 minutes, or until fork tender, stirring and turning halfway through baking.

Makes 6 servings.

Sweet Potato Casserole

ingredients

SWEET POTATOES

4 sweet potatoes

½ cup packed brown sugar

1 cup milk

2 eggs

1½ teaspoons vanilla extract

1 teaspoon salt

½ teaspoon pumpkin pie spice

TOPPING

1 cup packed brown sugar

⅓ cup all-purpose flour

3 tablespoons butter, melted

1 cup pecans

directions

Preheat the oven to 375 degrees. Grease a baking dish.

For the sweet potatoes, scrub the sweet potatoes, pierce with a fork and bake them for 35 to 45 minutes until fork tender. Lower the oven temperature to 350 degrees.

Cut open the sweet potatoes and scoop the flesh into a large bowl. Add the brown sugar, milk, eggs, vanilla extract, salt and pumpkin pie spice. Use a potato masher or immersion blender to mash, leaving some larger pieces for for texture. Spoon into the baking dish.

For the topping, combine the brown sugar and flour in a bowl. Sprinkle over the sweet potato mixture. Pour the butter over the sugar mixture. Cover with the pecans. Bake for 30 minutes until warm and golden brown.

Makes 6 to 8 servings.

Eggs Oglethorpe

An indulgent brunch dish of corncakes, hollandaise, eggs and fried green tomatoes—they'll hardly notice it's meatless.

ingredients

4 Cornmeal Cakes (page 72)

1 recipe Blender Hollandaise Sauce (page 166)

2 green (unripe) tomatoes, sliced

Salt to taste

¼ teaspoon black pepper

¼ teaspoon white pepper

½ teaspoon garlic powder

1 cup all-purpose flour

1 cup milk

2 cups Cajun-style fish fry mix or other cornmeal coating mix

Vegetable oil or bacon drippings for frying

4 poached eggs

¼ cup chopped fresh chives

directions

Keep the prepared Cornmeal Cakes warm in a warm oven. Set the Blender Hollandaise Sauce in a warm place.

Salt the tomato slices lightly. Set on paper towels to drain for at least 30 minutes. Combine the black pepper, white pepper and garlic powder. Sprinkle over the tomatoes. Put the flour, milk and fish fry mix in separate plates or shallow bowls. Dip each tomato slice into the flour, then the milk, and then the cornmeal coating.

Pour enough oil in a wide, shallow skillet to cover the bottom. Heat over medium-high heat until the oil shimmers. Add the green tomatoes slices in batches and fry for about 3 minutes on each side, or until browned. Keep warm in the oven.

To assemble, set a cornmeal cake on each plate. Top with a slice of fried green tomato, then a poached egg. Cover with Hollandaise Sauce. Garnish with chives to serve.

Makes 4 servings.

how to poach an egg

Did you know that you can poach eggs ahead of time and warm to temperature just before serving? Poach eggs by bringing a saucepan ¾ full of water to a boil with 1 tablespoon white vinegar. Reduce to a simmer. Crack eggs one by one into a shallow cup. WIth the lip of the cup touching the simmering water, gently pour the egg into the water. Remove with a slotted spoon after 4 minutes; blot briefly on a towel and serve immediately. If making ahead, remove after 3½ minutes and place in a bowl of warm water. When preparing to serve, return the poaching liquid to a simmer and let the eggs warm for about a minute before serving. You can poach the eggs the night before or the morning of the brunch. If it's already close to serving time, you can also hold fully poached eggs in a bowl of warm water, so you can do several batches of eggs and serve them all at once.

Cornmeal Cakes

ingredients

2 cups plain white or yellow cornmeal

1 teaspoon kosher salt

1 teaspoon baking soda

1 cup buttermilk

1 large egg, lightly beaten

¼ cup canola oil, divided

1 green onion, thinly sliced

directions

Combine the cornmeal, salt and baking soda in a small bowl. Combine the buttermilk, egg and 2 tablespoons of the oil in another bowl. Add the cornmeal mixture and stir just until blended. Add the green onions and mix lightly.

Brush 1 tablespoon of the remaining oil over a hot grill. Spoon ¼-cup portions of the batter onto the griddle. Flatten to about ½-inch thickness. Cook for 1½ to 2 minutes on each side, or until golden. Repeat with the remaining batter and oil.

Makes about 12 corncakes.

Tybee-Sunday's Brunch Casserole

ingredients

8 slices bacon, chopped

1 cup chopped onion

1 cup chopped green bell pepper

1 cup thinly sliced mushrooms

4 cups cubed day-old white bread

2 cups (8 ounces) shredded
   Cheddar cheese

10 eggs, lightly beaten

4 cups milk

1 teaspoon dry mustard

1 teaspoon sea salt

½ teaspoon onion powder

½ teaspoon black pepper

1 cup grape tomatoes

directions

Cook the bacon in a large pan until crisp. Drain on paper towels. Drain all but 1 tablespoon of the drippings from the pan. Cook the onion and bell pepper in the drippings over medium heat until the onion is tender. Add the mushrooms and continue cooking until their liquid is released.

Generously butter a 13 x 9-inch baking dish. Arrange the bread cubes in the bottom of the dish. Sprinkle the cheese over the bread. Top with the vegetables.

Beat the eggs, milk, dry mustard, salt, onion powder and pepper in a bowl until well blended. Pour over the vegetables. Sprinkle with the bacon and tomatoes. Cover and chill in the refrigerator for at least 8 hours.

Preheat the oven to 325 degrees. Uncover the dish and bake for 1 to 1½ hours, or until set. Tent with foil if the top begins to over brown.

Makes 6 to 8 servings.

Cheese Grits Soufflé

ingredients

2 teaspoons salt

4 cups water

1 cup quick-cooking grits (not instant)

2 cups (8 ounces) shredded
   Cheddar cheese

4 tablespoons (½ stick) butter

3 eggs

1 cup milk

Cayenne pepper to taste

directions

Preheat the oven to 350 degrees. Grease a 2-quart glass baking dish.

Bring the salt and water to a boil in a large saucepan. Add the grits and reduce the heat to medium-low. Cook, stirring occasionally, for about 5 minutes. Add the cheese and butter as the grits thicken, stirring to combine. Remove from the heat.

Beat the eggs and milk lightly together in a bowl. Add to the grits, stirring to combine. Season liberally with cayenne pepper to taste. Pour the mixture into the baking dish. Bake for 35 to 40 minutes, or until set.

Makes 6 to 8 servings.

Red Rice

This is the easiest and tastiest version we've tried of the popular Low Country side dish, which goes well with seafood and Mexican food.

ingredients

1 tablespoon olive oil

1 small onion, diced

1 cup long-grain rice, rinsed (optional)

6 slices bacon, cooked and crumbled

1 garlic clove, minced

½ cup canned diced or crushed tomatoes
   (or canned tomatoes with chiles)

1½ cups chicken stock

1 teaspoon salt

directions

Heat the oil in a deep saucepan over medium heat. Sauté the onion, stirring frequently, until translucent but not brown. Add the rice and bacon and sauté for a few minutes longer, stirring constantly so the rice doesn't brown. Add the garlic and sauté for 30 seconds. Add the tomatoes, stock and salt. Bring to a boil, reduce the heat, and then cover and simmer for 14 minutes. Remove the lid right away to prevent overcooking and to allow excess moisture to escape. Let stand for 5 minutes before stirring.

Makes 4 servings.

SEAFOOD

MONTEREY SQUARE, MONTEREY WARD — 1847

Monterey Square and ward were named in celebration of America's victory in the Mexican-American War (1846–1848) and to honor the Battle of Monterey, at which the second *USS Savannah* frigate figured prominently on July 7, 1846. The U.S. captured Monterey without firing one shot, thus, annexing California.

The last along the Bull Street promenade, Monterey Square and Monterey Ward are often referred as the city's most perfect. Their excellent condition can be attributed to Savannah's early historic preservation efforts, led by the Historic Savannah Foundation (at the time a community partner of the Junior League of Savannah). In 1967, these efforts saved the integrity of the ward and some of Savannah's most prestigious homes from their intended demolition in the name of improvement. Threatened buildings included the Armstrong House, Hugh-Mercer House, Mills B. Lane House, and the Brantley House.

Monterey Ward's exceptional buildings provide the backdrop for Monterey Square and Savannah's second obelisk. The original cornerstone was laid by General Lafayette in Chippewa Square in 1825 and was relaid 30 years later in Monterey Square. The idea was to keep the obelisks as far apart from each other as possible so that each would present a dramatic effect and not be diminished by the other. Robert E. Launitz designed the 50-foot monument from 1853-1855 in testament to Count Casmir Pulaski, a champion for freedom and independence in Poland and during the American Revolutionary War. He was mortally wounded in the Siege of Savannah in 1779. Pulaski's remains are reported to be reinterred under the monument in 1855 and 2005.

Photo courtesy of the Georgia Historical Society

Literacy has been a major focus for the Junior League of Savannah over the years. Member Augusta Clay reads aloud to children in 1942.

opposite page: *Liberty crowns the monument to Count Casimir Pulaski in Monterey Square.*

Low Country Boil

ingredients

½ cup Old Bay seasoning

1 or 2 bags Zatarain's crab boil

4 lemons, cut into halves

4 Vidalia onions, cut lengthwise into halves

1 pound new potatoes, cut into halves

2½ pounds smoked kielbasa

8 ears fresh corn, shucked and snapped in half

5 pounds (large or jumbo) fresh head-on shrimp or 4 pounds head-off shrimp

directions

Combine 4 quarts of water, the Old Bay and crab boil in an 8- to 10-quart pot. Bring to a boil. Add the lemons, onions and potatoes and cook at a low boil for about 5 minutes. Add the sausage and corn and boil for 6 to 8 minutes.

Add the shrimp and boil for 1 minute. Turn off the heat and let stand for 4 to 5 minutes until the shrimp just turn pink. Remove from the heat and drain liquid, or remove the shrimp, corn, potaotes, sausage, lemons and onions with a slotted spoon.

Serve in a bowl or mound on a paper-covered table.

Notes: The recipe doubles, triples and quadruples well for cooking in batches over large outdoor burners. Take care not to overfill the pot. If some guests are allergic to shellfish, cook a batch separately for them without the shrimp. For a small group, using vegetable stock or seafood stock for some or all of the boiling liquid will intensify the flavors.

Makes 8 large servings.

Shrimp and Grits

ingredients

4 cups chicken stock or water

1 cup heavy whipping cream

12 ounces (3 sticks) unsalted European-style butter, divided

1 cup stone-ground grits

Salt and freshly ground black pepper

1 cup diced tasso ham or cooked and crumbled bacon

¼ cup (1 ounce) freshly grated Parmigiano Reggiano cheese, plus more for garnish (optional)

6 ounces shredded mild or medium Cheddar cheese, plus more for garnish (optional)

2 tablespoons canola oil

2 tablespoons minced shallot or yellow onion

1 to 2 pounds fresh Georgia wild-caught shrimp, peeled and deveined

2 garlic cloves, minced

⅓ cup dry white wine

Creole seasoning to taste

1 lemon wedge

¼ cup chopped flat-leaf parsley

½ cup thinly sliced green onions

directions

Combine the chicken stock, cream and 4 tablespoons of the butter in a heavy-bottomed saucepan and bring to a simmer. Whisk in the grits and season with salt and pepper. Bring to a simmer and cook until mixture begins to thicken, whisking constantly to avoid sticking and burning. Stir in the ham. (If using bacon, add later.) Cook for 45 to 50 minutes, stirring often, until the grits are tender and thick. Stir in the Parmigiano Reggiano and Cheddar cheeses and the bacon, if using. Taste and adjust the seasoning.

Heat a large sauté pan over medium-high heat. Add the oil and shallots and sweat briefly. Add the shrimp and sauté for 2 to 3 minutes until almost cooked through. Add the minced garlic and cook, stirring occasionally, until the garlic is fragrant. Add the wine and stir, scraping up any brown bits. Add a good pinch of Creole seasoning, a squeeze of lemon and the parsley. Remove the pan from the heat. Add the remaining butter and cook until it is barely melted and the sauce is thick.

To serve, divide the grits among 4 soup plates. Spoon the shrimp mixture over the grits. Sprinkle with the green onions and garnish with additional cheese, if desired.

Makes 4 servings.

Shrimp Creole

Shrimp Creole, a quintessential New Orleanian dish, balances the richness of shrimp fat (from the heads) with the acidity of good tomatoes. The dish is best when both are in season.

ingredients

4 pounds (20- to 25-count) shrimp with heads and shells, or 3½ pounds larger shrimp

3 or 4 peppercorns

3 bay leaves, divided

¼ cup bacon drippings or chicken fat

¼ cup all-purpose flour

2 cups finely chopped onions

½ cup chopped green onions

1¼ cups finely chopped celery with leaves

1¼ cups finely chopped bell peppers

3 garlic cloves, minced

6 ounces tomato paste

8 ounces canned tomato sauce

1 teaspoon dried thyme

1 teaspoon dried basil

Salt, black pepper, white pepper and cayenne pepper to taste

2 cups peeled and diced ripe tomatoes (in season), or 1 (16-ounce) can low-salt tomatoes, chopped, with liquid

1 teaspoon Tabasco sauce

1 teaspoon lemon juice

3 tablespoons chopped fresh parsley

4 cups hot cooked rice

directions

Rinse and peel the shrimp, reserving the heads and shells. Refrigerate the shrimp. Combine the shrimp shells and heads with enough water to cover in a 2-quart saucepan. Add the peppercorns and 1 bay leaf. Bring to a boil. Reduce the heat to a simmer and cook for 20 to 30 minutes. Strain the shrimp stock into a measuring cup. This recipe requires 2 cups; the rest may be refrigerated or frozen for later use.

Heat the bacon drippings in a 4-quart saucepan over high heat. Add the flour and mix well. Cook, stirring often, over medium heat until the mixture is medium or dark brown. Add the onions, green onions, celery, bell peppers, garlic and remaining 2 bay leaves and cook over medium heat for 25 to 35 minutes until the onions are translucent. Add the tomato paste and cook, stirring, for 3 minutes. Add the tomato sauce, thyme, basil and a few tablespoons of the shrimp stock. Season with the salt, black pepper, white pepper and cayenne pepper to taste. Cook over medium-high heat for 5 minutes.

Add the tomatoes and the remaining stock. Bring to a low boil and stir, scraping the bottom of the pan. Reduce the heat to low and simmer, uncovered, for 1 hour, stirring occasionally.

Add the shrimp and cook until they are just barely pink, about 5 minutes. Add the Tabasco, lemon juice and parsley. Serve over hot cooked rice.

Note: White rice can be boiled like pasta in lots of salted water for about 14 minutes until cooked through, then drained and steamed, covered, in a colander over a pot of simmering water until ready to serve.

Makes 8 to 10 servings.

Grilled Shrimp with Black Bean Cakes and Corn and Tomato Salsa

ingredients

TOMATO SALSA

2 ears corn, cooked and kernels cut from the cobs

1 medium tomato, peeled and chopped

½ cup chopped sweet onion

1 jalapeño pepper, seeded and chopped

¼ cup chopped green bell pepper

Cilantro (optional)

1 tablespoon lime juice

Salt and black pepper to taste

BLACK BEAN CAKES

1 (15-ounce) can black beans, drained

1 medium onion, chopped

1 egg, beaten

½ cup seasoned bread crumbs

½ teaspoon ground cumin

1 cup all-purpose flour

¼ cup cornmeal (optional)

Vegetable oil for frying

SHRIMP

1 pound medium shrimp

Olive oil for brushing

Salt and black pepper to taste

1 lime

directions

For the tomato salsa, combine all of the salsa ingredients in a bowl. Mix well and let stand at least 1 hour before serving.

For the black bean cakes, combine the beans, onion, egg, bread crumbs and cumin. Shape the mixture into 3-inch patties. Coat both sides with flour, or a mixture of flour and cornmeal. Heat 2 to 4 tablespoons vegetable oil in a shallow sauté pan until the oil shimmers. Fry the patties in batches over medium-high heat, turning once, until both sides are browned. Set on a paper towel–lined baking sheet in a 200-degree oven until ready to serve.

For the shrimp, peel the shrimp, leaving the tail tips on for presentation if desired. Thread the shrimp onto skewers, about 5 to 8 shrimp per skewer. Brush with olive oil and season lightly with salt and pepper.

Prepare a medium-hot fire in the grill. Grill the shrimp for 2 to 4 minutes per side, or until the shrimp are just cooked through. Top black bean cakes with the grilled shrimp, and then with the salsa. Squeeze lime over the top and serve.

Makes 3 to 4 servings.

Grilled Marinated Shrimp

ingredients

3 tablespoons olive oil

2 tablespoons tomato paste

¼ cup red wine vinegar

1 teaspoon chopped garlic

½ teaspoon salt

1 teaspoon dried basil

1 teaspoon red pepper flakes

1 pound shrimp

directions

Combine the olive oil, tomato paste, vinegar, garlic, salt, basil and pepper flakes in a medium bowl. Peel and devein the shrimp. Add to the marinade and stir to coat. Marinate for 20 to 30 minutes. Thread the shrimp onto skewers and grill for 1 to 2 minutes per side, just until the shrimp turn pink.

Shrimp and Pasta

ingredients

directions

PASTA AND SAUCE

1 pound fettuccine

8 tablespoons (1 stick) butter, softened

1 cup (4 ounces) finely grated
    Parmesan cheese

1 cup heavy whipping cream

1 teaspoon salt

¼ teaspoon cayenne pepper, or to taste

SHRIMP

8 tablespoons (1 stick) butter, melted

1 yellow bell pepper, cut into
    thin slices

1 red bell pepper, cut into
    thin slices

1 bunch green onions, white and green
    parts chopped separately

2 garlic cloves, chopped

½ pound mushrooms, sliced

2 pounds large fresh head-off,
    shell-on shrimp, or 3 pounds head-on,
    shell-on shrimp

1 cup halved grape tomatoes

1 cup frozen peas or 1-inch pieces
    asparagus, cooked al dente

Grated Parmesan cheese for serving

For the pasta and sauce, cook the pasta in boiling salted water for 18 to 20 minutes until al dente, and then drain. Keep warm. Combine the butter, Parmesan cheese, cream, salt and cayenne pepper in a large serving bowl.

While the pasta is cooking, make the shrimp. Heat the butter in a large skillet and sauté the red and yellow bell peppers and the white parts of the onions. Sauté until tender. Add the garlic, mushrooms and shrimp and sauté until shrimp are almost cooked through. Add the tomatoes and peas and mix well.

Add the warm drained pasta to the large bowl with the cheese mixture and toss until well combined. Arrange the shrimp on the pasta. Sprinkle with the green portion of the green onions and extra Parmesan cheese. Serve immediately.

Note: This recipe halves well. Serve with a green salad and toasted French or sourdough bread.

Makes 8 servings.

Oysters Catherine

ingredients

½ pound bacon

½ cup (2 ounces) grated Romano cheese

½ cup seasoned bread crumbs or
plain bread crumbs seasoned with
¼ teaspoon dried thyme, ¼ teaspoon
dried oregano and a dash of dried basil

1 tablespoon butter

½ bunch green onions, chopped

4 sprigs parsley, chopped

4 garlic cloves, chopped

1 (12-ounce) bag frozen quartered
artichoke hearts, thawed

Juice of ½ lemon

1 pint oysters in their liquor

½ teaspoon salt

¼ teaspoon black pepper

¼ teaspoon white pepper

Dash of cayenne pepper

Lemon juice and/or chicken stock,
if needed

directions

Cook the bacon in a skillet until crisp. Drain on paper towels. Drain all but 2 tablespoons of bacon drippings from the skillet. Crumble the bacon and combine with the Romano cheese and bread crumbs in a bowl.

Preheat the oven to 400 degrees. Grease an au gratin dish or 4 to 6 individual ramekins.

Melt the butter with the bacon drippings and sauté the green onions, parsley and garlic until tender but not browned. Add the artichoke hearts and lemon juice and sauté for 5 minutes. Add the oyster liquor, salt, black pepper, white pepper and cayenne pepper. If there's more than ¾ cup liquid, cook to reduce the liquid to ¾ cup total. Lower the heat to a simmer.

Fold in the oysters and simmer briefly. Add all but 3 to 4 tablespoons of the bread crumb mixture. Turn carefully to combine. The mixture should be wet but not liquid. If it seems too dry, add a bit of lemon juice and/or chicken stock. Spoon the mixture into the prepared au gratin pan or ramekins. Sprinkle with the remainder of the bread crumb mixture.

Bake for 10 to 12 minutes, or until bubbly and browned on top. Serve wtih French bread and a green salad for a meal.

Makes 6 appetizer servings or 4 main course servings.

Linguine with Smoked Salmon

ingredients

3 tablespoons butter, divided

½ cup sliced green onions

½ cup peeled, seeded and chopped tomato (optional)

1 tablespoon lemon juice

¼ cup dry white wine

1 tablespoon tomato paste

1 cup heavy whipping cream

Freshly ground black pepper to taste

½ to 1 cup coarsely chopped smoked salmon

8 ounces linguine

2 tablespoons chopped fresh parsley, basil or dill

directions

Heat 2 tablespoons of the butter in a skillet over medium heat. Add the green onions and sauté until tender. Add the tomato and cook briefly. Add the lemon juice and wine and cook until reduced by a third.

Stir in the tomato paste and cream. Cook over medium-low heat until the sauce is slightly reduced and beginning to thicken. Add the pepper and salmon.

Cook the linguine in stockpot of boiling salted water until al dente. Drain and toss with the remaining 1 tablespoon of butter in a large warmed bowl. Pour the salmon sauce over the linguine and toss to coat. Sprinkle with the parsley. Serve immediately.

Note: Freshly cooked salmon also works well.

Makes 4 servings.

Shad and Roe

ingredients

1 lemon, cut in half

1 shad, filleted

Salt, black pepper, paprika and white pepper to taste

2 pairs shad roe

4 slices bacon, at room temperature

1 tablespoon butter

directions

Preheat the oven to 400 degrees. Squeeze half the lemon over the shad. Season lightly with salt, black pepper, white pepper and paprika.

Wrap each roe with a slice of bacon. Secure with wooden picks. Arrange the fish and roe in a greased glass baking dish. Bake for 10 minutes. Turn the heat to broil. Baste the fish with pan juices. Broil until browned.

Remove the fish from the pan and continue broiling the roe until the bacon is crisp, turning once to broil both sides. Squeeze the other lemon half over the fish before serving.

Note: Bacon-wrapped roe may be cooked separately in a frying pan, though cooking it with the fish lends flavor to the dish.

Makes 4 to 6 servings.

shad roe history

This delicate fish with its one-of-a-kind roe hails locally from the Ogeechee River. According to fishermen, when the forsythia blooms, the shad are in the river. When the shad start their run from the ocean to fresh water, it is a sign that winter is ending and spring is coming. Shad is a sweet-tasting fish, and in the South, shad and its roe are commonly served for breakfast. Most years, the shad catch remains available until late March to mid-April, and occasionally into May. Savannahians enjoy them while they can!

Shad has an important place in American history as well as on the American table. For example, shad saved George Washington's army from starvation at Valley Forge. The hungry troops were saved by a big shad run in the spring of 1778 on the Schuylkill River.

Pan-Seared Grouper with Lemon Butter Pan Sauce

ingredients

1 teaspoon sweet paprika

1 teaspoon salt

½ teaspoon garlic powder

¼ teaspoon cayenne pepper

¼ teaspoon white pepper

¼ teaspoon black pepper

¼ teaspoon dried thyme

¼ teaspoon dried oregano

2 (6-ounce) pieces grouper or
    other firm fish

1 tablespoon all-purpose flour

1 to 2 tablespoons vegetable oil

½ cup dry white wine

2 tablespoons lemon juice

1 cup fish stock or seafood stock

2 tablespoons butter

directions

Preheat the oven to 400 degrees. Combine the paprika, salt, garlic powder, cayenne pepper, white pepper, black pepper, thyme and oregano in a small bowl. Pat the fish dry and season liberally with the paprika mixture. Just before cooking, dust the fish with the flour.

Heat the oil in an oven-safe pan over medium-high heat until the oil shimmers. Add the fish and cook for 4 minutes until the fish browns and begins to release from the pan. Turn and cook for 3 to 4 minutes on the other side. If the fish isn't firm, continue cooking in the oven—total cooking time will depend on the thickness of the fish, about 8 minutes total cooking time per 1 inch of thickness. Transfer the fish to warm plates, reserving the pan juices.

Return the pan to medium-high heat. Pour in the wine and lemon juice and heat, scraping up any browned bits from the pan. Add the stock and bring to a boil. Reduce the heat and simmer, adding any accumulated liquid from the fish, until the sauce is reduced by half.

Raise the heat to high. Add the butter, 1 tablespoon at a time, and shake the pan vigorously to incorporate and emulsify the sauce. Divide and pour the sauce over the two fish portions. Serve immediately.

Makes 2 servings.

Crabmeat Au Gratin

This may possibly be the best thing you ever eat in your life. It's even more decadent with jumbo lump crabmeat.

ingredients

2 tablespoons plus
    2 teaspoons butter, divided

¼ cup chopped green onion

1 tablespoon chopped fresh parsley

¼ cup heavy whipping cream

2 tablespoons milk

1 tablespoon cognac

¼ teaspoon salt

¼ teaspoon white pepper

½ pound lump crabmeat

1 cup (4 ounces) shredded sharp
    Cheddar cheese

Cayenne pepper to taste

directions

Preheat the oven to 375 degrees. Grease 2 au gratin dishes or ramekins.

Heat 2 tablespoons of the butter in a skillet and sauté the green onions and parsley until tender. Add the cream, milk, cognac, salt and white pepper and mix well. Heat through. Remove the pan from the heat and add the crabmeat, mixing just to blend. Return the skillet to the heat and heat through.

Divide half of the crab mixture among the prepared dishes. Top with half of the cheese, and then the remaining crab mixture. Finish with the remaining cheese. Dot with the remaining 2 teaspoons butter. Dust with cayenne pepper.

Bake for 14 to 16 minutes until bubbly. Set the heat to broil. Broil for 1 to 2 minutes until browned.

Note: To make entrée-size portions, use 12 ounces of crabmeat, double the remaining ingredients and use 1½ cups cheese. Serve with good crusty French bread, a green salad and Champagne!

Makes 4 appetizer portions.

Crab Cakes

ingredients

1 large egg

¾ teaspoon Worcestershire sauce

¾ teaspoon lemon juice

¾ teaspoon seafood seasoning, such as Old Bay

¾ teaspoon Dijon mustard

½ cup mayonnaise

½ pound backfin crabmeat

1 pound lump or jumbo lump crabmeat

¼ cup chopped fresh parsley

¾ cup crushed butter crackers

directions

Combine the egg, Worcestershire sauce, lemon juice, seafood seasoning, mustard and mayonnaise in a bowl. Combine the crabmeat, parsley and cracker crumbs in another bowl, mixing lightly to combine. Add the egg mixture to the crab mixture and mix lightly. Shape into 5-ounce cakes. Broil, bake or pan-fry until browned on both sides.

Makes 6 crab cakes.

grades of crabmeat

Crabmeat is sold in four major grades, each of which can be used to best advantage:

1. *Jumbo lump crabmeat: large nuggets of crab, the most costly variety, and the best for au gratins, crab salads, and other dishes that showcase premium crabmeat.*

2. *Lump/Backfin lump: Lump crabmeat has the same flavor and texture as jumbo lump but is in smaller pieces. Use lump when you don't necessarily need jumbo pieces, such as in crab cakes, benedict, pasta and risotto dishes.*

3. *Backfin or special crabmeat is ideal for crab cake recipes that have multiple ingredients, such as bisques, chowders, and other appetizers.*

4. *Claw crabmeat is the "dark meat" of the crab. It's very flavorful and mixes nicely with lump/backfin lump. Try it in crab tacos!*

POULTRY

REMAINING ORIGINAL SQUARES

Oglethorpe's first six wards, laid out on his two visits to the colony in 1733 and 1736, spanned Bay Street to the north, South Broad Street (now known as Oglethorpe Avenue) to the south, and ran east to west from Lincoln Street to Jefferson Street. Six squares, or marketplaces, were planned in the wards; the last of these to be built honors Oglethorpe himself. Savannah's southward expansion advanced incrementally into the original City Commons through the nineteenth century within Oglethorpe's original east and west boundaries.

ELLIS SQUARE, DECKER WARD — 1733

Savannah's third square, laid out in 1733, was named in honor of Sir Henry Ellis, who became the second Royal Governor of Georgia in 1757 and led the province in relative harmony compared to his predecessor, Governor Reynolds. In 1763, the City Market was relocated from Wright Square to Ellis Square. During the Revolutionary War, coffee, sugar, tea, and flour were no longer found in the market. Cornmeal took the place of flour, and bacon became the staple food of the day. After Savannah's great fire in 1820 (intensified by ignited gunpowder stored in the square, then known as Market Square), the market was moved to South Broad Street (which was temporarily renamed Market Street) until citizen outcry returned the market to its time-honored spot in Ellis Square. The small wooden building was replaced by a brick structure in the 1850s and replaced again in 1872 by a large brick edifice designed by Augustus Schwabb.

Hucksters' calls of "oyster by' 'er," "'yers swimp," "ay shota fish," and "watermelons so sweet, don't need no meat" announced the seafood, vegetables, and fruit for sale. Savannah's market culture, the building, and the square itself were destroyed in 1954 to build a multi-story parking deck for nearby merchants. This development served as the impetus for Savannah's historic preservation movement. By the time the fifty-year lease on the property expired, the climate had shifted toward more thoughtful development in the historic district. The parking structure was demolished and Ellis Square was reclaimed and redesigned for the twenty-first century, complete with underground parking, interactive fountains, and gathering spaces.

TELFAIR SQUARE, HEATHCOTE WARD — 1733

Established in 1733, Telfair Square was the fourth square laid out by Oglethorpe. The original site of the Royal Government House, Telfair Square was originally named "St. James" in

opposite page: The Reverend John Wesley presides over Reynolds Square.

honor of the palace of St. James in London. The Revolutionary War victory led to the square's renaming to honor the Telfair family for its services and contributions to the city of Savannah.

The last descendant in a long line of distinguished ancestors, Mary Telfair was a generous philanthropist who funded artistic, literary, and social causes throughout Savannah. Miss Telfair's brother, Alexander, built a beautiful mansion on the square, which she inherited after his death, then deeded to the city upon her death. In 1866, the Georgia Historical Society opened Telfair Academy of Arts and Sciences in the mansion. The Telfair is the oldest art museum in the Southeast.

REYNOLDS SQUARE, REYNOLDS WARD — 1734

Reynolds Square was established in 1734 as the fifth of Oglethorpe's original six squares and honors Captain John Reynolds, who was appointed the first royal governor of the colony of Georgia after the original 21 trustees relinquished their interests to the Crown. Although he was a valiant sea commander, Reynolds proved to be a most unpopular governor. Remarkably, the square named for him continued to serve as the center of Savannah government after his recall. On August 10, 1776, the Declaration of Independence was delivered by express messenger to the House of Assembly in Reynolds Square—the first place in the state of Georgia where the founding document of the United States of America was read.

The monument featured in the middle of the square is a tribute to Reverend John Wesley, father of the eighteenth-century Methodist movement and Savannah's third Church of England chaplain. Savannah is the location of the second known meeting of the Methodists, held in 1736, and it was in this city that Wesley established the nation's first Sunday school at Christ Church and wrote his hymnal. Savannah was Charles and John Wesley's only American parish.

OGLETHORPE SQUARE, ANSON WARD — 1742

General James Edward Oglethorpe (1696-1785) was the leader of the humanitarian experiment that conceived of and founded the Georgia colony. At his headquarters in a tent under four Bay Street pine trees, Oglethorpe negotiated for, laid out, and established the City of Savannah. For eleven years, Oglethorpe was Georgia's head of government and commander-in-chief. When Savannah was threatened by the presence of Spanish forces in St. Augustine in 1736, Oglethorpe led troops and colonists to establish the town of Frederica (in honor of Frederick, King George II's only son) on St. Simon's Island. Upon his return to Savannah, Oglethorpe laid out this last square before his final departure in 1743. An extraordinary man, Oglethorpe never returned to Georgia, but in his lifetime, he saw the infant colony grow into an independent state in a new country.

The Owens-Thomas House is located on the Northeast trust lot of Oglethorpe Square and is one of America's best residential examples of regency architecture. William Jay, a notable architect from Bath, England, was commissioned by Richard Richardson in 1817 to design his residence, and it was from the home's balcony that the Marquis de Lafayette addressed the citizens of Savannah in 1825. In 1951, the Owens-Thomas House was willed to the Telfair Academy of Arts and Sciences. The site currently operates as a historic house museum with an extensive collection of Owens family furnishings, period art and décor, and the nation's best-preserved urban slave quarters in the original carriage house.

Sweet Tea-Brined Fried Chicken

ingredients

½ gallon plus 2 cups (10 cups total) sweet tea, divided

⅓ cup plus 2 tablespoons salt, divided

1 (3 to 4-pound) whole chicken, cut into pieces

2 cups whole buttermilk

2 tablespoons hot red pepper sauce

3 cups all-purpose flour

1 teaspoon black pepper

½ teaspoon ground red pepper

5 cups canola oil

directions

Combine ½ gallon of the tea and ⅓ cup of the salt in a large, nonreactive container. Stir until the salt dissolves. Add the chicken pieces. Cover and refrigerate for at least 8 hours.

Preheat the oven to 350 degrees. Spray the rack of a broiler pan with nonstick cooking spray. Set the rack in the pan.

Combine remaining 2 cups of sweet tea with the buttermilk and hot sauce in a bowl. Combine the flour, remaining 2 tablespoons of salt, black pepper and red pepper in a shallow dish.

Remove the chicken from the brining liquid. Dip each piece into the buttermilk mixture, then coat with the flour mixture. Place on a wire rack. Coat each piece in flour mixture again, shaking off the excess. Return to the wire rack.

Heat the oil in a large cast iron skillet until a deep-fry thermometer reads 350 degrees. Cook the chicken in batches, starting with the dark meat, then the white meat, then the giblets. Cook, turning occasionally, for 5 to 8 minutes until golden brown on all sides. Adjust the heat as needed to maintain oil at 350 degrees. Place the chicken on the broiler rack. Bake for 10 to 20 minutes, or until a meat thermometer inserted into the thickest portion of the chicken reads 165 degrees.

Makes 4 servings.

tips for deep-frying without a thermometer

Don't have a kitchen thermometer? No problem. Oil that is ready for frying will bubble around the stick end of a wooden spoon inserted into the oil. If your oil begins to smoke, you know it's too hot. Frying oil will cool with the addition of food at room temperature, so you may need to adjust the heat until it comes back to the desired temperature.

Pan-Fried Chicken Breast with Lemon Caper Butter

ingredients

Vegetable oil for frying

4 small boneless skinless chicken breasts, pounded thin

Salt, black pepper and cayenne pepper to taste

½ cup all-purpose flour

1 to 2 cups panko (crisp Japanese bread crumbs)

1 egg beaten with 2 tablespoons water

½ cup chopped Vidalia onion

1 garlic clove, minced

1 cup dry white wine

1 cup chicken stock

Zest and juice of ½ lemon, in separate bowls

2 ounces water

½ bunch green onions, chopped

1 tablespoon capers

8 tablespoons (1 stick) butter

1 tablespoon chopped fresh parsley

1 bunch watercress (optional)

Olive oil for drizzling

directions

Pour enough oil to to come ½ inch up the side of a large skillet and set over medium heat. Season the chicken with salt, black pepper and cayenne pepper. Put the flour, egg and panko in 3 shallow bowls. Coat the chicken with flour, shaking off the excess. Dip the chicken into the egg, allowing the excess to drip back into the bowl. Finally, coat the chicken with panko.

Fry the chicken in the oil on both sides until browned and cooked through. Remove to a plate or keep warm in the oven. Drain the oil from the pan.

Heat the water in the pan and add the onion and garlic. Sauté until tender. Add the wine, stock and lemon juice and cook until reduced by two-thirds. Add the zest, green onions and capers. Add the butter, whisking it into the liquid as it bubbles until a pan sauce forms. Whisk in the parsley.

To serve, set a chicken portion on each plate. Drizzle 2 tablespoons of the sauce over the chicken and around each plate. Arrange a large handful of watercress on each piece of chicken. Drizzle olive oil over the watercress.

Makes 4 servings.

Southwest Chicken

ingredients

2 teaspoons coarse salt

1 teaspoon cracked black pepper

1½ teaspoons paprika

½ teaspoon chili powder

½ to 1 teaspoon cayenne pepper

½ teaspoon ground cumin

¼ teaspoon ground coriander

1 (3½-pound) frying chicken, quartered, or 4 leg quarters

Red, yellow and green bell peppers, cut into halves

directions

Combine the salt, black pepper, paprika, chili powder, cayenne pepper, cumin and coriander in a small bowl. Rinse the chicken and pat dry. Rub the spice mixture all over the chicken pieces, making sure to include the joints. Cover and refrigerate for 1 to 2 hours.

Prepare a medium or low fire in a grill. Grill the chicken, turning often, for 35 to 45 minutes, or until cooked through. Add the bell peppers to the grill for the last 10 minutes of cooking the chicken.

Makes 4 servings.

Ginger-Curry Chicken Thighs

ingredients

1 tablespoon finely grated fresh ginger

2 tablespoons lime juice

2 teaspoons curry powder

1 bunch green onions, finely chopped

1 teaspoon salt, plus extra for seasoning

1 teaspoon black pepper, plus extra for seasoning

8 bone-in, skin-on chicken thighs

directions

Preheat the broiler.

Combine the ginger, lime juice, curry powder, green onions, salt and pepper in a small bowl. Pat the chicken dry and arrange on a baking sheet. Season the chicken with salt and pepper. Loosen the skin of each thigh and rub one-eighth of the seasoning mixture under the skin of each piece. Turn the pieces skin-side down on the baking sheet. (For unusually large pieces, make a small ½-inch slit in the meat on each side of the leg bone.)

Broil the chicken 4 inches from the heat for 5 minutes. Turn and broil for 6 to 8 minutes longer, or until the skin is crisp. Serve with the pan juices.

Note: To make a sauce from the pan juices, pour off most of the fat from the roasting pan. Pour the juices into a skillet, scraping up the browned bits and adding them to the skillet. Cook over high heat until the mixture begins to sizzle. Add 3 tablespoons lime juice and 1 cup chicken stock or coconut milk and cook, stirring up the browned bits, until the mixture boils. Add any juice from the resting chicken thighs. Cook until reduced by about one-third. Swirl in 1 tablespoon of butter to finish.

Makes 6 to 8 servings.

Chicken Curry

ingredients

2½ pounds chicken breast tenderloins

Salt, black pepper and cayenne pepper
to taste

¼ cup all-purpose flour

5 tablespoons butter, divided

1 medium onion, minced

2 garlic cloves, minced

2 bell peppers, diced

3 tablespoons curry powder

1 (15-ounce) can stewed tomatoes

1 (13-ounce) can coconut milk

Dash of Worcestershire and Tobasco sauce

directions

Season the chicken with salt, black pepper and cayenne pepper to taste. Coat lightly with flour and shake off excess.

Heat 3 tablespoons of the butter in a skillet over medium-high heat. Add the chicken and cook until browned on all sides. Remove the chicken from the skillet. Reduce the heat to medium.

Preheat the oven to 350 degrees. Heat the remaining butter in the skillet and sauté the onion, garlic and bell peppers for 5 to 7 minutes until tender, stirring frequently. Stir in the curry powder and cook for 2 to 3 minutes longer. Stir in the tomatoes and coconut milk. Heat to a simmer. Stir in the Worcestershire and Tabasco sauces, salt and pepper. Arrange the chicken in an 8-inch square glass baking dish. Pour the sauce over the chicken. Bake for 45 minutes.

Makes 4 to 6 servings.

Fiesta Chicken

ingredients

2 tablespoons Taco Seasoning (page 167)

1 cup Cheddar cheese crackers, crushed

4 bone-in, skin-on chicken breast halves

1 bunch green onions, finely chopped

2 tablespoons butter

2 cups heavy whipping cream

1 cup chicken stock

1 cup (4 ounces) shredded Mexican
cheese blend

1 (4-ounce) can green chiles, drained
and chopped

directions

Preheat the oven to 350 degrees. Grease a 13 x 9-inch baking dish. Combine the taco seasoning and cracker crumbs on a plate. Coat the chicken with the crumb mixture. Arrange the chicken in the baking dish.

In a small saucepan, sauté the green onions in the butter until tender. Add the cream, chicken stock, cheese and chiles. Bring to a simmer and cook for 1 to 2 minutes. Pour over the chicken. Bake for 45 minutes or until tender. Serve with rice, beans, salsa, pico de gallo and any other festive condiments that you like.

Makes 4 servings.

Braised Chicken with Artichokes and Tomatoes

This dish is a nice, light taste of spring, and with a couple of easy stopping points so it can be started in advance and finished as company arrives. It's easy and healthy enough for a weeknight dinner timed well to serve a group of 4 to 6 people. Serve with green beans, salad and brown rice or pasta.

ingredients

3 tablespoons all-purpose flour

Salt, black pepper and cayenne pepper
    to taste

8 skinless bone-in chicken thighs, or
    4 boneless, skinless breasts, cut in half,
    or a combination

2 tablespoons olive oil or vegetable oil

4 garlic cloves, slivered

1 shallot, slivered, or ¾ to 1 cup sliced
    green onions

1 cup dry white wine

1 cup chicken stock

3 tablespoons lemon juice

12 to 16 ounces frozen artichoke hearts,
    thawed and drained

1 cup cherry tomatoes, cut into halves

1 tablespoon chopped fresh basil

1 sprig fresh thyme, chopped,
    or ¼ teaspoon dried thyme

2 tablespoons chopped fresh parsley

directions

Season the flour with salt and black pepper. Pat the chicken dry, then season lightly with salt, black pepper and cayenne pepper. Coat the chicken lightly with the seasoned flour, shaking off the excess.

Heat the oil in a large skillet over medium-high heat until it shimmers. Cook the chicken (in batches if necessary) for 3 to 5 minutes per side or until browned. Remove to a plate. Pour off all but a few tablespoons of drippings from the skillet.

Reduce the heat to medium and add the garlic and shallot. Sauté for 5 to 7 minutes until tender. Increase the heat to medium-high and add the wine, stock and lemon juice. Cook for 1 to 2 minutes, scraping any browned bits from the bottom of the pan and incorporating into the sauce.

Reduce the heat to medium, add the artichokes and mix well. Add the tomatoes and herbs.

Return the dark meat to the pan. Cover and simmer for 10 minutes. Return the white meat to the pan and spoon with liquid. Cover and simmer for 10 minutes longer. Adjust the seasoning before serving.

Makes 4 to 6 servings.

White Chicken Spinach Lasagna

ingredients

9 lasagna noodles

8 tablespoons (1 stick) butter

1 onion, chopped

8 garlic cloves, minced, divided

½ cup all-purpose flour

1 teaspoon salt

2 cups chicken broth (see page 101)

1½ cups milk

4 cups (16 ounces) shredded
    Italian-blend cheese, divided

1 cup (4 ounces) grated
    Parmesan cheese, divided

1 tablespoon Italian seasoning

½ teaspoon black pepper

2 cups ricotta cheese

½ teaspoon salt

2 cups chopped cooked chicken meat

2 (10-ounce) packages frozen chopped
    spinach, thawed and squeezed dry

1 tablespoon chopped fresh parsley

directions

Preheat the oven to 350 degrees. Grease a 13 x 9-inch baking dish. Boil the noodles in a large pot of lightly salted water for 8 to 10 minutes. Drain and rinse with cold water.

While the noodles are boiling, melt the butter in a large saucepan over medium heat. Cook the onion and 2 of the garlic cloves in the butter, stirring frequently, until tender. Stir in the flour and salt and simmer until bubbly. Add the broth and milk and boil, stirring constantly, for 1 minute. Stir in 2 cups of the Italian-blend cheese and ¼ cup of the Parmesan cheese. Stir in the Italian seasoning and pepper. Remove from the heat.

Combine the ricotta cheese, the remaining 6 garlic cloves and salt in a bowl.

Spread one-third of the cheese sauce over the bottom of the baking dish. Layer with one-third of the noodles, then the ricotta mixture, and then chicken. Make another layer of noodles. Top with one-third of the cheese sauce, and then the spinach. Top with the remaining 2 cups of Italian-blend cheese and ½ cup of Parmesan cheese.

Arrange the remaining noodles over the cheese. Spread the remaining cheese sauce evenly over the noodles. Sprinkle with parsley and the remaining ¼ cup Parmesan cheese. Bake for 35 to 40 minutes, or until browned and bubbly.

Makes 8 to 10 servings.

Chicken Pot Pie

This recipe can be made in a 2-quart casserole, or divided among two shallow pie plates or four to six ramekins.

ingredients

2 tablespoons butter

1 medium-size white onion, chopped

1 cup chopped celery

1 cup chopped carrot

1 garlic clove, minced

¼ cup all-purpose flour

½ cup milk

2 cups chicken stock (see below)

¼ teaspoon salt

½ teaspoon black pepper

4 cups shredded cooked chicken
   (about 2 pounds boneless chicken,
   or 1 rotisserie chicken)

2 teaspoons dried thyme,
   or 2 tablespoons fresh thyme

1 cup frozen peas or butterbeans

1 egg whisked with 1 tablespoon water

1 to 2 sheets Basic Pie Dough (page 134)

directions

Preheat the oven to 425 degrees.

Heat the butter in a large saucepan over medium-high heat. Add the onion, celery and carrots and sauté until the onion is translucent and the vegetables are tender. Add the garlic and sauté for about 1 minute, but do not let the garlic brown. Add the flour and cook for 2 minutes, stirring constantly. Stir in the milk, stock, salt and pepper. Bring to a boil. Reduce the heat to medium and simmer for 10 minutes, stirring occasionally, until the mixture coats the back of a spoon. Add the chicken, thyme and frozen peas. Taste and adjust the seasoning.

Pour the mixture into 2 shallow pie dishes, a 2-quart casserole or other ovenproof dishes. Top with the pastry. Bake for 35 minutes, or until crust is browned.

Makes 4 to 6 servings.

quick stock

Homemade stock/bone broth is more flavorful and nutritious than store bought, and it's simple to make. This quick stock is a great time saver if you don't have time to make a rich, slow-cooked stock.

Combine the bones from a home-roasted or store-bought rotisserie chicken and enough water to cover in a pot. Add a bay leaf and 3 or 4 peppercorns. If onion ends, carrot pieces, or celery ends are handy, add them to the pot as well and bring to a boil. Let simmer at least 10 minutes and up to several hours. Strain through a colander, and then through a fine mesh strainer. Use immediately, store covered in the fridge for up to a week, or freeze for future use.

Stuffed Chicken Thighs with Red Pepper Tomato Sauce

ingredients

RED PEPPER TOMATO SAUCE

1 tablespoon extra-virgin olive oil

2 garlic cloves, minced

1 dried bay leaf

1 large red bell pepper, diced

1 (28-ounce) can tomato purée

1 handful fresh oregano leaves

Salt and black pepper to taste

STUFFING

3 garlic cloves

1 handful fresh oregano leaves

1 (6-ounce) jar pitted Kalamata
olives, drained

5 tablespoons extra-virgin olive oil

CHICKEN

20 small or 12 to 15 large skinless boneless
chicken thighs

Salt to taste

directions

Preheat the oven to 375 degrees. Cover a baking sheet with parchment paper.

Combine all of the sauce ingredients in a medium saucepan. Bring to a boil then reduce the heat to a simmer. Simmer, uncovered, as the stuffed thighs are prepared.

For the stuffing, combine all the stuffing ingredients in the bowl of a food processor. Pulse until a paste forms.

For the chicken, lay the chicken pieces on a work surface skin-side up. Season with salt. Flip, skin-side down, and season with salt. Top each thigh with 1 to 2 teaspoons of the stuffing, and roll to enclose the stuffing. Arrange the thighs, loose-edge down, on the prepared baking sheet. Bake for 30 minutes, or until cooked through.

Clean the bowl of the food processor. Pour the sauce into the bowl. Let cool for at least 10 minutes. Process until smooth, then return to the saucepan. Keep warm over low heat.

Serve the chicken topped with a dollop of sauce.

Makes 8 servings.

Chicken and Wild Rice Casserole

The South Carolina Lowcountry Sustainers are an active group of more than 200 members who live on Hilton Head Island and in the surrounding areas of Bluffton, Okatie, Beaufort, Ridgeland, Dataw Island, and Callawassie Island. This casserole has been served at the Lowcountry Sustainers Transfer luncheon for years.

ingredients

½ cup chopped onion

8 ounces mushrooms, sliced

8 tablespoons (1 stick) butter

¼ cup all-purpose flour

1½ cups chicken stock
  (see page 101)

1½ cups half-and-half

6 ounces wild rice, cooked

3 cups chopped cooked chicken

½ cup toasted almonds, chopped

2 tablespoons chopped fresh parsley

½ cup diced red bell pepper

½ cup diced green bell pepper

1 teaspoon salt

½ teaspoon black pepper

directions

Preheat the oven to 350 degrees. Grease a 2-quart shallow baking dish.

Sauté the onion and mushrooms in the butter in a large saucepan until tender. Stir in the flour and cook for 2 minutes. Stir in the stock and half-and-half. Cook, stirring continuously, until thickened. Remove from the heat; the sauce will seem thin.

Add the rice, chicken, almonds, parsley, red bell pepper, green bell pepper, salt and pepper and mix well. Pour into the baking dish. Cover and bake for 30 minutes. Uncover and bake for 15 minutes longer, or until hot in the center. (If using a deeper casserole dish, bake uncovered for the entire 45 minutes.)

Makes 4 to 6 servings.

MEAT & GAME

EAST SIDE SQUARES, PART 1

Emerging from the Revolutionary War, Savannah rebuilt and expanded, enlarging the pattern of wards, squares, and streets, many of which were named after war heroes. Post-Revolutionary Savannah was characterized by an increasing population, refinement, hospitality, wealth, religious, and educational progress, governance, and the promise of peace and stability.

WARREN SQUARE, WARREN WARD — 1791

Warren Square was the first extension of the city after Oglethorpe's departure from Savannah. Established in 1791, this square was named for General Joseph Warren, who recruited Paul Revere and William Dawes to spread the alarm of British troops and ultimately fell at the Battle of Bunker Hill during the Revolutionary War. Today, Savannah's smallest square is surrounded by many homes that were moved from their original locations, including the houses at 22 Habersham Street, 24 Habersham Street, 404 East Bryan Street, and 426 East Julian Street.

WASHINGTON SQUARE, WASHINGTON WARD — 1790

In 1790, Washington Square was laid out and named in honor of George Washington, first president of the United States. Originally known as Firehouse Square because of the firehouse located in the center, Washington Square was the site of Savannah's New Year's Eve bonfire until 1954. All year, mischievous young boys would 'go hooking' and raid garbage cans and backyards to collect kindling, stashing the materials in many of the square's underground water reservoirs. Then on New Year's Eve, the fire ring was trenched, the structure was constructed, and gas was spread, so that at midnight, when the city's bells rang out, the fire would be lit and flames would roar throughout the night's celebrations.

GREENE SQUARE, GREENE WARD — 1799

This square, laid out after the Revolutionary War, honors Major-General Nathanael Greene, hero of the Southern front and second in fame and command only to General George Washington. For his service, Georgia awarded him the largest loyalist confiscated plantation, Mulberry Grove Plantation, located just north of the city near Port Wentworth. After Greene's premature death in 1786, his widow, Catherine Littlefield Greene, solicited the assistance of Eli Whitney, who invented the cotton gin on its grounds (at her suggestion, some say).

opposite page: Residents of Washington Square (pictured), center of Savannah's Irish population, established the Hibernian Society and in 1826 hosted Savannah's first Saint Patrick's Day Parade.

COLUMBIA SQUARE, COLUMBIA WARD — 1799

Similar to our nation's capital, Columbia Square (established 1799) is named for Columbia, the original female personification of the United States of America and perhaps its most recognizable symbol until the Statue of Liberty was erected. Since the 1947 formation of the Columbia Square Association, Columbia Ward has successfully preserved a building from every period of Savannah's architecture. The proposed demolition of the Isaiah Davenport tenement house (1820) sparked formation of the Historic Savannah Foundation and a preservation effort that has since saved more than 300 of Savannah's architectural treasures.

Eudora and Wainwright Roebling renovated Columbia Square in the 1970s in honor of Eudora's parents, Augusta and Wymberly DeRenne. The Roeblings relocated a fountain from the historic Wormsloe Plantation, the home of one of Georgia's first settlers, Noble Jones, to mark the center of the square.

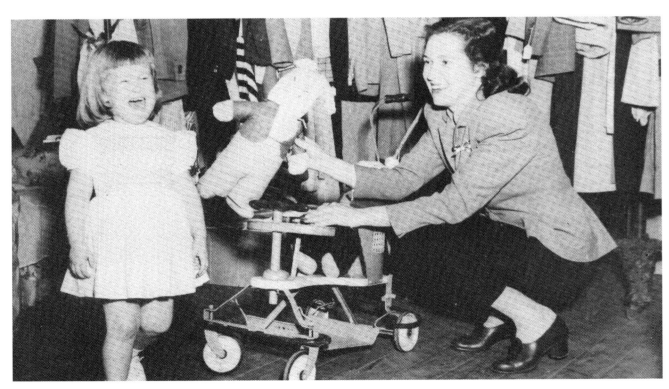

Sometimes children do NOT want to part with a toy when a mother wants to donate that toy to Thrift Sale! Here, Addine Leitch is not a cheerful giver about parting with her doll to volunteer Louise Lynch at the 1949 Junior League of Savannah's Thrift Sale.

Mrs. Wilkes' Dining Room Meat Loaf

You don't have to wait in line for this meat loaf, made famous at Mrs. Wilkes' Boarding House.

ingredients

2 eggs

2 pounds ground chuck

2 cups crushed corn flakes

¾ cup minced onion

¼ cup minced green bell pepper

2 tablespoons soy sauce

2 teaspoons salt

1 tablespoon dry mustard

¼ cup milk

1 (10.5-ounce) can cream of
   mushroom soup

directions

Preheat the oven to 350 degrees. Beat the eggs with a fork in a large bowl. Add the beef, corn flake crumbs, onion and bell pepper and mix lightly. Combine the soy sauce, salt, dry mustard, milk and soup and mix well. Add to the meat, mixing well but lightly. Form the meat mixture into an oval loaf in a glass baking dish. Bake for 50 to 70 minutes or until cooked through.

Makes 6 servings.

mrs. wilkes

Mrs. Wilkes' Dining Room is a part of the heritage of Savannah. "In 1943, a young Sema Wilkes took over a boarding house in historic downtown Savannah. Her goal was modest: to make a living by offering comfortable lodging and homestyle Southern cooking served family style in the downstairs dining room." Southern food lovers from all over the world continue to show up for lunch, where you can find platters of meat loaf and cornbread dressing, sautéed yellow squash, mashed potatoes and gravy, beef stew, biscuits, and more.

Grilled Leg of Lamb

Because of its natural tenderness, lamb is ideal for grilling, but a butterflied leg (particularly a large one) is rather unwieldy on the grill. Placing one or two metal skewers through the meat lengthwise and a couple crosswise will not only make the lamb easier to turn, but will help you "bunch up" the meat to create a more even thickness across the butterflied meat. If you have access to a large rosemary bush, dried rosemary branches impart a smoky rosemary flavor that beautifully complements grilled lamb.

ingredients

2 lemons

5 garlic cloves, minced

⅓ cup finely chopped fresh Italian parsley

1 tablespoon chopped fresh rosemary

2 tablespoons olive oil, plus more for coating the meat

Kosher salt and freshly ground black pepper to taste

1 (4-pound) boneless leg of lamb, netting removed

directions

Finely grate the zest from the lemons. (Or remove strips with a vegetable peeler, then finely chop the strips.) Combine the zest, garlic, parsley, rosemary and 2 tablespoons olive oil in a medium bowl. Season with salt and pepper. Stir to an evenly combined paste.

Unroll the lamb, lay it flat on a cutting board and remove any large pieces of gristle, sinew or fat. Season the top of the lamb generously with salt and pepper. Spread the lemon mixture over the meat with your hands. Roll to enclose the seasoning. Tie with butcher's twine in several places, 1 to 2 inches apart. Insert 2 to 4 metal skewers through the meat, one or two lengthwise and one or two crosswise. Rub olive oil, salt and pepper all over the outside of the meat. Set it on a tray in the refrigerator.

An hour before cooking, remove the lamb from the refrigerator and let it come to room temperature. Light a hot fire in a grill. Lightly oil the grill rack.

Grill the lamb with the lid down, turning every 15 minutes or so, for 35 to 45 minutes until it reaches an internal temperature of 125 to 130 degrees on an instant-read thermometer. Let rest on a cutting board for 20 minutes. Remove the twine to carve the lamb.

Note: Instead of rolling up the meat into a tied roast, the butterflied leg of lamb may be cooked flat on the grill, provided it has been evenly butterflied. Cooking time is reduced significantly.

Makes 6 to 8 servings.

Marinated Pork Tenderloins

ingredients

¼ cup olive oil

3 tablespoons soy sauce

3 tablespoons red wine vinegar

3 tablespoons lemon juice

1 tablespoon Worcestershire sauce

2 garlic cloves, minced

1 tablespoon chopped fresh parsley

1½ teaspoons black pepper

2 pork tenderloins

directions

Combine the olive oil, soy sauce, vinegar, lemon juice, Worcestershire sauce, garlic, parsley and pepper in large ziptop storage bag. Add the pork and seal the bag. Marinate for at least 4 hours in the refrigerator.

Prepare a fire in a grill, or preheat the oven to 450 degrees. Grill, uncovered, or oven-roast for 15 to 20 minutes until the meat reaches 160 degrees.

Makes 6 servings.

Caribbean Glazed Pork Tenderloin

ingredients

RUB

1 teaspoon chili powder

1 teaspoon cumin

1 teaspoon cinnamon

2 teaspoons garlic salt

1 teaspoon black pepper

PORK

1 pork tenderloin

2 tablespoons olive oil, or more for grilling

GLAZE

1 cup light brown sugar

4 garlic cloves, chopped

1 tablespoon hot red pepper sauce

directions

Preheat the oven to 350 degrees.

For the rub, combine all the rub ingredients in a small bowl. Rub all over the tenderloin. Heat the olive oil in a large, oven-safe pan over medium heat. Add the pork and sear for 5 minutes, turning until all sides are seared.

While the pork is searing, make the glaze. Combine the brown sugar, garlic and hot sauce in a small bowl. Press onto the seared pork, coating all sides as best you can.

Roast the tenderloin for 20 minutes, or until the meat reaches 150 degrees. Cover and let stand for 10 minutes before slicing.

Makes 2 to 3 servings.

Dry-Rubbed Smoked Ribs

This rub works as beautifully on brisket as it does on ribs.

ingredients

2 pounds light brown sugar

2½ tablespoons black pepper

2 tablespoons salt

3 tablespoons dried parsley flakes

2 tablespoons seasoned salt

Nutmeg to taste

¼ cup garlic powder

2 tablespoons lemon pepper seasoning

Red pepper to taste

Ribs, about 3 to 4 ribs per person

Watermelon Barbecue Sauce (page 165) or favorite barbecue sauce (optional)

directions

Combine the brown sugar, black pepper, salt, parsley flakes, seasoned salt, nutmeg, garlic powder, lemon pepper and red pepper in a large bowl and mix well. The recipe makes a large quantity of rub. Use on ribs or brisket as needed and store the rest in an airtight jar.

Generously sprinkle the mixture onto all sides of the ribs and rub into the meat. Let stand at room temperature for at least an hour. (Or wrap the ribs in plastic wrap and refrigerate for 8 hours or longer.)

Preheat a smoker to 250 degrees. Add wood chips or chunks to the smoker according to the manufacturer's directions. Smoke the meat for 2 hours, adding wood chips as needed. Remove the ribs from the smoker and wrap in heavy-duty aluminum foil. Cook for 2 hours longer.

Remove the ribs from the foil and return to the smoker for 15 minutes, basting with Watermelon Barbecue Sauce, if desired.

Note: Alternatively, ribs can be roasted in the oven. Line a rimmed baking sheet with aluminum foil and set a wire rack on top. Arrange the ribs on the rack in a single layer, meaty side up. Broil under high heat until the rub browns and sizzles. Reduce the heat to 300 degrees and move the ribs to the center rack of the oven. Roast for 2½ to 3 hours, covering with aluminum foil halfway through cooking. Mop with sauce, if desired, and cook until tender.

Beef Tenderloin

ingredients

4 to 5 pounds beef tenderloin

2 tablespoons olive oil

2 tablespoons black pepper

2 tablespoons garlic powder

1½ teaspoons salt

2 to 4 tablespoons Worcestershire sauce

Quick Marchand de Vin (page 164)
  or your favorite béarnaise sauce

directions

Let the tenderloin come to room temperature. Preheat the broiler.

Rub the tenderloin with the olive oil. Combine the pepper, garlic powder and salt in a small bowl and rub all over the meat to create a crust. Sprinkle with the Worcestershire sauce.

Broil the meat on a broiler pan for 25 minutes, turning once halfway through cooking. Remove from the oven and immediately cover with foil. Let stand for 2 hours before slicing. Slice to serve.

Makes 10 to 12 servings.

Photo courtesy of the Georgia Historical Society

A Volkswagen Bug and donkey decoration were used to drive the streets of Savannah to promote the 1959 Junior League of Savannah's Thrift Sale.

Moroccan Spiced Beef with Couscous

ingredients

1 tablespoon olive oil

2 medium carrots, cut in ¼-inch dice, or precut matchstick carrots

1 medium onion, diced

1 tablespoon paprika

1 teaspoon allspice

½ teaspoon cinnamon

1 pound ground beef

1 (15-ounce) can garbanzo beans, drained

½ cup chopped dried apricots

1 cup chopped fresh parsley

1½ teaspoons salt

2 cups chicken stock or beef stock, divided

1 (12- to 13-ounce) box couscous

directions

Heat the olive oil in a large skillet over medium heat. Add the carrots, onion, paprika, allspice and cinnamon and sauté for 10 minutes. Add the beef and cook, stirring, until browned and crumbly. Drain the fat from the skillet. Add the beans, apricots, parsley, salt and ¾ cup of the stock to the skillet. Simmer for 10 minutes or until slightly thickened.

Prepare the couscous according to the package directions, substituting the remaining 1¼ cups of the stock for some of the water. Serve the beef mixture over the couscous.

Makes 6 to 8 servings.

Venison Tenderloin

This versatile preparation can be served with a simple pan sauce, below, or with the Quick Marchand de Vin sauce (page 164).

ingredients

1 garlic clove, minced

1 tablespoon fresh lemon juice

1 tablespoon olive oil

1 tablespoon Dijon mustard

1 bay leaf, crushed

1 teaspoon dried rosemary

½ teaspoon black pepper

1 (1-pound) venison tenderloin

directions

Combine the garlic, lemon juice, olive oil, mustard, bay leaf, rosemary and pepper in a small bowl and mix well. Set the venison in a rectangular baking dish and pour the marinade over the top. Turn to coat all over. Cover the dish with plastic wrap and refrigerate for at least 8 hours

Preheat the oven to 450 degrees. Sear the venison in a hot oven-safe pan over high heat for 3 to 4 minutes per side. Transfer to the oven and roast for 15 minutes. Let stand for 10 minutes. Cut into thin slices and arrange on a serving platter. Drizzle with sauce to serve, if desired. (See note below.)

Note: To make a quick pan sauce while the meat rests, heat the pan used for searing the venison over medium heat. Pour in ½ cup red wine and 1 tablespoon lemon juice. Cook, stirring and scraping up the browned bits, until reduced. Add 1 cup stock or water, stirring to combine. Bring to a boil over high heat. Cook until reduced by about one-fourth, adding any pan juices from the resting tenderloin. Turn off the heat and swirl in 2 tablespoons butter, shaking the pan back and forth to emulsify the sauce. Serve immediately.

Makes 2 to 3 servings.

Venison Shoulder with Spiedi Seasoning

The marinade mixture is good on venison, lamb and other red meat as well.

ingredients

2 to 3 tablespoons roasted garlic

2 cups canola oil

1 teaspoon oregano

2 teaspoons meat tenderizer

Salt and black pepper to taste

½ cup dry red wine

1 tablespoon red pepper flakes

½ cup water

1 tablespoon lemon juice

Finely chopped parsley to taste

1 (6- to 7-pound) venison shoulder
  or leg roast

directions

Combine the garlic, canola oil, oregano, meat tenderizer, salt, pepper, wine, red pepper flakes, water, lemon juice and parsley in a large bowl or pot and mix well. Add the venison, turning to coat. Transfer all the venison and marinade to a 2-gallon ziptop plastic bag. Marinate for 3 days, turning the bag at least twice a day.

When ready to cook, remove the meat from the bag. Wrap it in two layers of heavy-duty aluminum foil. Prepare a fire in a grill. Grill over indirect heat for 3½ hours. Remove the foil and grill for 30 minutes longer.

Makes 8 servings.

Venison Roast with Red Wine and Roasted Garlic

ingredients

Salt and black pepper to taste

1 or 2 venison roasts

2 tablespoons olive oil

6 carrots, chopped

1 onion, chopped

Minced garlic to taste (optional)

1 cup dry red wine

2 tablespoons all-purpose flour

½ teaspoon dried oregano

½ teaspoon dried basil

½ teaspoon dried parsley

¼ teaspoon paprika

Pinch of cayenne pepper

¼ teaspoon celery seeds

¾ teaspoon onion powder

1 bulb garlic, roasted

1 cup beef stock or chicken stock

3 sprigs rosemary

½ pound new potatoes

12 mushrooms

½ cup warm water, optional

directions

Preheat the oven to 350 degrees. Rub salt and pepper all over the venison. Heat the olive oil in a Dutch oven over medium-high heat. Sear the venison on all sides. Remove from the pan.

Sear the carrots in the pan. Add the onion and minced garlic, if desired, and sauté until the onion is translucent. Remove from the pan. Pour in the wine and stir to deglaze.

Combine the flour, oregano, basil, parsley, paprika, cayenne pepper, celery seeds and onion powder in a small bowl and mix well. Add the flour mixture to the pan, along with the roasted garlic, squeezed from the bulbs. Mix well. Add the stock and rosemary.

Return the vension and cooked vegetables to the pan. Add the potatoes and mushrooms. Cover and bake for 20 minutes per pound until the internal temperature reaches 140 for medium-rare. Remove the venison to a platter. Tent with foil for 10 to 20 minutes before slicing.

Note: To make a sauce, set the Dutch oven over medium-high heat and add ½ cup warm water, scraping up any browned bits from the bottom of the pan with a wooden spoon . Return to the oven for 10 to 20 minutes while the venison rests. After slicing, pour the juices from the serving platter into the sauce. Cook, stirring, over medium heat until hot. Serve with the roast.

Makes 8 servings.

Venison with Blackberry Sauce

ingredients

1 cup dry red wine

3 tablespoons Dijon mustard

Salt and freshly ground black pepper
 to taste

1 (1-pound) venison tenderloin
 or backstrap

2 tablespoons butter

1 tablespoon olive oil

2 cups chicken stock

3 tablespoons blackberry jam

directions

Combine the wine and mustard in a nonreactive dish large enough to hold the venison. Rub salt and pepper into the venison. Add to the mustard mixture, turning to coat. (Alternatively, the tenderloin can be cut into 1-inch slices before being combined with the mustard mixture.)

Refrigerate for at least 6 hours, turning every couple of hours. Remove the venison from the mustard mixture and shake off any excess.

Heat the butter and olive oil in a large sauté pan over medium heat. Brown the tenderloin for about 5 minutes per side until cooked to rare. Remove from the pan and tent with foil. The meat will continue to cook.

To make the blackberry sauce, add the chicken stock to the pan immediately, scraping and swirling to deglaze. Cook until reduced by half. Add the blackberry jam and cook for about 5 minutes or until the mixture thickens.

Cut the tenderloin into 1-inch slices (if not already cut) and serve drizzled with the blackberry sauce.

Makes 2 to 3 servings.

Quail or Dove in Wine

ingredients

4 to 6 quail or dove

Salt to taste

Flour for coating

4 tablespoons (½ stick) butter

½ cup chopped mushrooms

½ cup chopped Vidalia onion

½ cup chicken stock

½ cup white wine

1 tablespoon chopped fresh parsley

½ cup heavy whipping cream

Hot cooked wild rice

directions

Preheat the oven to 350 degrees. Wash and dry the birds. Rub with salt and flour. Sauté lightly in the butter in a medium pan, then remove to an enamel-coated cast iron casserole or skillet or other oven-safe skillet.

Sauté the mushrooms and onions in the butter remaining in the sauté pan. Add the stock and wine, scraping the bottom with a wooden spoon and swirling to deglaze the pan. Stir in the parsley and pour over the birds.

Bake, uncovered, for 30 minutes, basting frequently. Remove the birds from the casserole.

Heat the cream and pour it into the casserole. Set the dish over medium heat and cook for 5 to 10 minutes, or until the liquid reduces and thickens enough to coat the back of a spoon. Pour the sauce over the birds to serve.

Makes 2 to 3 servings.

CAKES, PIES & PUDDINGS

EAST SIDE SQUARES, PART 2

CRAWFORD SQUARE, CRAWFORD WARD —1841

Crawford Square was established in 1841 to honor William H. Crawford, governor of Georgia from 1843 to 1847 and United States Secretary of War from 1847 to 1850. Crawford was a two-time U.S. presidential nominee (1816 and 1824) and the only Georgian to run for president until Jimmy Carter. The current design of the square dates from 1968-1972.

TROUP SQUARE, TROUP WARD — 1851

George Michael Troup, Georgia governor (1823-1827) and U.S. senator, was commemorated by the construction of the square in 1851. Residential in nature, its eastern lots were developed with row houses fronting each other. The square fell into neglect and vehicle emergency lanes were run through it. Neighborhood revitalization in the 1960s was made possible through a partnership between the Historic Savannah Foundation and the U.S. Department of Housing and Urban Development offering the first urban renewal loans for rehabilitation. The square was restored in 1969 and the central armillary sphere records Savannah's relative celestial position.

The Unitarian Church is the only public building found on a Troup trust lot. Built with financing from Moses Eastman, the Unitarian Church was originally located on Oglethorpe Square. The Unitarian church's music director, James Pierpont, composed "Jingle Bells" in 1857. The Civil War diminished Savannah's Unitarian Association and an African American Episcopalian church purchased the church, renamed it, and shifted the building to its present location on Troup Square. The building was later re-purchased by the Unitarian Church. Each year the congregation blesses the pets of Savannah, which sip from the 1897 recast iron drinking fountain. Without its pedestal, the bowl can accommodate four-legged visitors.

WHITEFIELD SQUARE, WESLEY WARD —1851

Whitefield Square honors Wesley's successor, the Reverend George Whitefield, "the prince of pulpit orators" and the leader of the Great Awakening of 1740. In 1740, Whitefield founded Bethesda Orphan House and Academy, the nation's first orphanage, to honor the humanitarian aims of early settlers in Savannah.

The last Savannah square to be laid out, local lore states that beneath Whitefield Square and surrounding lands are the "Old Negro Burial Grounds," 1813-1853. Several bodies

opposite page: *The fountain in the middle of Lafayette Square was dedicated by the Colonial Dames of America.*

of prominent African Americans including Reverend Andrew Bryan and Reverend Henry Cunningham were reinterred in Laurel Grove cemetery; however, spirits of the un-exhumed are said to linger in the square.

CALHOUN SQUARE, CALHOUN WARD — 1851

John C. Calhoun, U.S. vice president under Presidents John Quincy Adams and Andrew Jackson, visited Savannah as Secretary of War to inspect the steamship *Savannah*, first steamship to cross the Atlantic, before its 1819 voyage to Liverpool. After its establishment in 1851, Calhoun Square was one of many squares that held May Day celebrations. Today, the Massie Heritage Center continues to host the tradition of the May Day Pole, around which young schoolchildren cavort and crown their king and queen. May Day traditions also once included the Military Ball at which Chatham Artillery Punch (page 163) was served to Savannah socialites. On the west side of the square is Wesley Monumental United Methodist Church, named in honor of Charles and John Wesley. Facing the west side of the square are the church's stained glass window portraits of the brothers. The sanctuary was completed in 1890.

LAFAYETTE SQUARE, LAFAYETTE WARD — 1837

The heroic Revolutionary War actions of General George Washington's compatriot, French General Marquis de Lafayette, were celebrated in America upon his return 50 years later. "Lafayette" enthusiasm was high as Savannah welcomed his national tour in 1825, and he was honored again when Lafayette Ward and Lafayette Square were laid out in 1837. Lafayette Square is crowned by the twin steeples and golden crosses of the Cathedral of St. John the Baptist, the oldest Roman Catholic Church in Georgia. This square also memorializes two of Savannah's female icons: prize-winning author Flannery O'Connor and Girl Scouts of the U.S.A. founder Juliette Gordon Low, who established scouting in Savannah in 1912.

Photo courtesy of the Georgia Historical Society

Over the years, the Junior League of Savannah has donated vehicles, water fountains, gardens, and even a pond! Here are league members with a new bus with a hydraulic lift to transport special needs children, donated to the Chatham County Schools Special Education Department in 1956.

Pear Almond Cake

ingredients

4 to 5 ripe juicy pears, the softer the better

8 tablespoons (1 stick) butter, softened

¾ cup plus 1 tablespoon sugar, divided

2 eggs

1 teaspoon vanilla extract

1 teaspoon almond extract

1 cup all-purpose flour

1 teaspoon baking powder

½ teaspoon salt

1 tablespoon amaretto or
   almond liqueur (optional)

directions

Preheat the oven to 350. Grease an 8-inch springform pan.

Peel and core the pears. Cut each into eight slices.

Beat the butter and ¾ cup of the sugar in a bowl with a mixer. Add the eggs one at a time, mixing well after each addition. Beat in the vanilla and almond extracts. Combine the flour, baking powder and salt. Add to the butter mixture gradually, beating just until combined. Do not overmix.

Pour the batter into the pan. Arrange the pears on top of the batter, flat-side down. Press the pears firmly into the batter, squeezing as many in as possible. Appearance doesn't matter, as the batter will cook up around the pears. Drizzle with the amaretto, then sprinkle with the remaining tablespoon of sugar.

Bake for 1 hour, or until the cake just barely tests done. Do NOT overbake; this cake is best when barely done or removed from the oven slightly underdone and allowed to finish as it cools.

Note: If you only have a 9-inch springform pan, prepare "one and a half" of the recipe: Use 6 pears, 1½ sticks butter, 3 eggs, etc.

Makes 8 to 12 servings.

the golden isles of georgia

Junior League of Savannah members who live in the Golden Isles area of Georgia (Brunswick and St. Simons , Little St. Simons, Jekyll and Sea Islands), complete a variety of projects with community agencies in their region selected through an application process. Recent projects have included St. Mark's Towers Retirement Community's Annual Christmas Dinner, CASA (Court Appointed Special Advocates) of Glynn County, and Morningstar Children and Family Services, Inc.

Chocolate Cake

ingredients

2 squares unsweetened chocolate

1 cup milk

4 eggs, separated

1¾ cups sugar

1 cup all-purpose flour

1 teaspoon baking powder

Glossy Chocolate Frosting (below)

directions

Preheat the oven to 350 degrees. Grease and flour a 13 x 9-inch pan. Melt the chocolate with the milk in the top of a double boiler set over simmering water. Cook, stirring constantly, for 5 minutes. Remove from the heat and let cool.

Beat the egg yolks lightly in a mixing bowl, and then stir in the sugar until smoothly blended. Add the chocolate mixture and mix well. Add the flour and baking powder.

Beat the egg whites in a metal bowl until they hold stiff peaks. Fold into the chocolate batter, and then pour into the prepared pan. Bake for 25 to 30 minutes, rotating halfway through baking time, until the cake tests done. Let cool completely before frosting with Glossy Chocolate Frosting below.

Makes 12 servings.

Glossy Chocolate Frosting

ingredients

6 tablespoons shortening

9 tablespoons baking cocoa

⅓ cup milk, warmed

¼ teaspoon salt

1 teaspoon vanilla extract

2 cups confectioners' sugar

Chopped nuts (optional)

directions

Melt the shortening in a saucepan over low heat. Stir in the cocoa, and then the warm milk; mix well. Add the salt, vanilla and confectioners' sugar and beat with an electric mixer until smooth. The frosting will thicken as it cools. If necessary, set the pan of frosting in a bowl of ice and water and beat until it reaches the desired consistency. Frost the cake, then top with chopped nuts if desired.

Caramel Cake with Caramel Icing

ingredients

CAKE

16 tablespoons (2 sticks) butter, softened

2 cups sugar

4 eggs

3 cups self-rising flour

1 cup buttermilk

2 teaspoons vanilla extract

CARAMEL ICING

3 cups sugar, divided

1 egg, lightly beaten

8 tablespoons (1 stick) butter

¾ cup evaporated milk

1 teaspoon vanilla extract

Extra evaporated milk or cream,
     for thinning

directions

For the cake, preheat the oven to 350 degrees. Butter and flour three 9-inch round cake pans.

Beat the butter until soft. Add the sugar and beat until creamy. Add the eggs one at a time, beating well after each addition. Beat in the flour and buttermilk alternately, one-third at a time, mixing well after each addition. Stir in the vanilla extract.

Divide the batter between the prepared pans. Bake for 20 to 25 minutes until the cakes test done. Turn onto a rack and cool completely before icing with the caramel icing.

To make the icing, combine 2½ cups of the sugar with the egg, butter and milk in a saucepan. Cook over low heat until the butter melts. Melt the remaining ½ cup sugar in a small cast iron skillet over low heat, cooking until it is brown and liquid. Watch closely as the sugar begins to liquefy—the mixture goes from brown to burned quickly. Add the caramelized sugar to the butter mixture and raise the heat to medium. Cook the mixture, stirring occasionally, for about 10 minutes until it reaches the soft ball stage (234 degrees on a candy thermometer), or until the mixture leaves the sides of the pan.

Remove from the heat. Let cool slightly, then add the vanilla. Beat with an electric mixer for up to 20 minutes or until thick enough to spread and cling to the cake. If the icing becomes too thick, thin with evaporated milk or cream

Makes 12 to 16 servings.

Palmetto Pink Cake

This pretty pink cake is a take on a standard white cake with buttercream icing. Fresh strawberries in both the cake and icing tint them pink.

ingredients

1 cup chopped strawberries

2 cups plus 1 teaspoon sugar

Salt

16 tablespoons (2 sticks) unsalted butter, softened

4 eggs

1 cup buttermilk

2 teaspoons vanilla extract

2½ cups all-purpose flour

1 teaspoon baking soda

1 teaspoon baking powder

Strawberry Butttercream Frosting (page 128)

directions

Combine the strawberries, 1 teaspoon of the sugar and a pinch of salt in a bowl and let stand for a few minutes until the strawberries release their juice.

Preheat the oven to 350 degrees. Grease and flour two 9-inch round cake pans, tapping out the excess flour.

Beat the butter in a mixer on medium-low speed. Add the remaining 2 cups sugar, gradually increasing the speed to medium-high. Scape down the side of the bowl. Beat in the eggs one at a time. Add the buttermilk and vanilla and mix just until combined.

Sift the flour, baking soda, baking powder and ½ teaspoon salt in a bowl and mix well. Add the dry ingredients to the butter mixture 1 cup at a time, mixing just until combined.

Drain and reserve the liquid from the strawberries to use in the Strawberry Buttercream Frosting (page 128). Gently fold the strawberries into the batter. Divide the batter between the cake pans. Bake for 25 minutes, or until the cakes test done. Cool in the pans for about 10 minutes. Turn out onto wire racks and cool completely before frosting between the layers and over the top and side of the cake with the Strawberry Buttercream Frosting.

Makes 12 to 16 servings.

Strawberry Buttercream Frosting

ingredients

16 tablespoons (2 sticks) unsalted butter, softened

1 teaspoon vanilla extract

Pinch of salt

4 cups confectioners' sugar

Strawberry juice (reserved from Palmetto Pink Cake, page 126)

Red food coloring (optional)

Milk, as needed

directions

Beat the butter in a stand mixer until light and fluffy. Add the vanilla and beat well. Add the pinch of salt. Add the confectioners' sugar, 1 cup at a time, beating well after each addition. The consistency will become very thick. Add enough strawberry juice to thin and flavor the frosting. Add a drop or two of food coloring, if desired.

If the icing is still too thick, beat in milk, 1 tablespoon at a time, until the desired consistency is reached.

Makes enough to frost one 2-layer cake.

Lemon Cake

ingredients

8 tablespoons (1 stick) unsalted butter, softened

1½ cups sugar

2 eggs, at room temperature

1½ teaspoons vanilla extract

2 cups all-purpose flour

1 tablespoon baking powder

1 teaspoon salt

1 (3-ounce) box lemon gelatin mix

1 cup milk

Zest and juice of 3 lemons

2 cups confectioners' sugar, plus extra for sprinkling

directions

Preheat the oven to 350 degrees. Generously grease and lightly flour a Bundt pan. Beat the butter and sugar in a bowl with an electric mixer until fluffy. Beat in the eggs one at a time. Stir in the vanilla. Sift the flour with the baking powder, salt and gelatin. Add to the butter mixture in batches alternately with the milk. Pour into the pan. Bake for 50 minutes. While the cake is baking, combine the lemon zest and juice with the confectioners' sugar to make a glaze.

Remove the cake from the oven and poke holes in the cake with a fork. Pour the lemon glazed over the cake. Let the cake stand for 15 minutes. Invert the cake onto a serving plate. Sprinkle with confectioners' sugar before serving.

Note: This cake may be baked and then frozen.

Makes 8 to 12 servings.

Graham Cracker Streusel Coffee Cake

ingredients

STREUSEL

9 full-size graham crackers, preferably whole wheat

1 cup brown sugar

¾ cup chopped pecans

¾ cup chopped walnuts

2 teaspoons cinnamon

¼ teaspoon nutmeg

11 tablespoons butter, melted

CAKE

2 cups all-purpose flour

2 teaspoons baking powder

¼ teaspoon salt

12 tablespoons (1½ sticks) unsalted butter, softened

1½ cups sugar

2 teaspoons vanilla extract

6 large egg whites

¾ cup milk

1 (3-ounce) package French vanilla pudding mix

directions

For the streusel, put the graham crackers in a ziptop bag, seal it and roll with a rolling pin to crush. Combine the crumbs with the brown sugar, pecans, walnuts, cinnamon and nutmeg in a large bowl. Add the 3 tablespoons melted butter and mix well.

For the cake, preheat the oven to 350 degrees. Grease a 13 x 9-inch baking pan. Combine the flour, baking powder and salt in a bowl and mix well. Beat the butter and sugar in the bowl of a mixer on medium speed for about 5 minutes or until very soft and light. Beat in the vanilla.

Whisk the egg whites and milk in a bowl until combined.

Beat one-fourth of the flour mixture into the butter mixture, scraping down the bowl. Add one-third of the milk mixture, stopping and scraping down the bowl. Beat in another fourth of the flour mixture, then another third of the milk mixture. Scrape again. Repeat with another fourth of the flour mixture and the remaining milk mixture. Mix in the remaining flour mixture. Add the pudding mix and beat until well combined.

Pour half the batter into the prepared pan. Sprinkle with half of the streusel mixture. Carefully spoon the remaining batter over the streusel. Top with the remaining streusel. Bake for 45 minutes for an aluminum pan, 30 to 35 minutes for a dark pan, or until the cake tests done.

Note: Baking the cake in an aluminum pan gives a better result, with edges that are less overbrowned

Makes 12 to 16 servings.

Apple Spice Cake

Bake the cake in either a 13 x 9-inch pan for easy serving, or a Bundt pan for a crisp crust and nice presentation.

ingredients

10.5 ounces (2 sticks plus 5 tablespoons) butter, softened

2 cups sugar

3 eggs

3 cups all-purpose flour

1 tablespoon cinnamon

½ teaspoon ground cloves

½ teaspoon freshly grated nutmeg

1 teaspoon baking soda

1 teaspoon salt

4 to 5 cups chopped unpeeled apples (about 4 large)

1 cup chopped pecans or walnuts

1 teaspoon vanilla extract

Confectioners' sugar (optional)

Vanilla ice cream, cinnamon ice cream or whipped cream, for serving

directions

Preheat the oven to 350 degrees. Grease and flour a 13 x 9-inch baking pan or Bundt pan. Beat the butter and sugar in a bowl until creamy. Beat in the eggs one at a time. Stir together the flour, cinnamon, cloves, nutmeg, baking soda and salt in another bowl. Add the dry ingredients to the butter mixture 1 cup at a time, blending well after each addition. Stir in the apples, pecans and vanilla. Pour into the prepared pan.

Bake for 60 to 70 minutes until the cake tests done. Let cool in the pan for 20 minutes. Turn out onto a wire rack to cool slightly. Sift confectioners' sugar over the top, if desired. Serve warm with vanilla or cinnamon ice cream, or let cool completely and serve with whipped cream.

Makes 10 to 12 servings.

Poppy Seed Cake

ingredients

5 eggs

3 cups all-purpose flour

2 cups sugar

1 tablespoon baking powder

½ cup milk

1 cup orange juice (not concentrate)

½ cup vegetable oil

¼ cup poppy seeds

1 teaspoon almond extract

directions

Preheat the oven to 375 degrees. Grease an angel food cake pan or Bundt pan.

Beat the eggs in a large bowl with an electric mixer. Add the flour, sugar, baking powder, milk, orange juice, oil, poppy seeds and almond extract. Beat for 5 minutes. Spoon into the prepared pan. Bake for 45 minutes, or until the cake tests done.

Makes 10 servings.

Traditional Pound Cake

Pound cake is perfect for bringing along on a holiday weekend or a beach outing, since it can be served for breakfast or dessert, by itself, toasted with butter or topped with Meyer Lemon Curd (page 141) and whipped cream.

ingredients

16 tablespoons (2 sticks) butter, softened

3 cups sugar

6 eggs, at room temperature

8 ounces sour cream, at room temperature

1 teaspoon vanilla extract

1 teaspoon almond extract

3 cups sifted cake flour

¼ teaspoon baking soda

directions

Preheat the oven to 350 degrees. Grease and flour a Bundt pan or 2 loaf pans.

Beat the butter and sugar with an electric mixer in a bowl until creamy. Add the eggs one at a time, beating well after each addition. Add the sour cream, vanilla extract and almond extract, and mix well. Sift the flour with the baking soda. Fold into the batter with a spoon or spatula.

Spoon the batter into the prepared pan (or 2 loaf pans). Bake for 1 hour and 15 minutes for a Bundt pan, or less for the loaf pans. Let cool slightly on a wire rack. Turn out and cool completely. Best made 1 to 2 days ahead of serving.

Makes 12 to 16 servings.

Ginger Peach Bourbon Pie

ingredients

½ recipe Basic Pie Dough (page 134)

FILLING

¼ cup bourbon

3 tablespoons cornstarch

½ teaspoon cinnamon

¾ teaspoon grated fresh ginger

2 teaspoons vanilla extract

5 cups sliced peeled peaches, or more for
a deep-dish pie (about 4 to 6 medium)

3 tablespoons brown sugar

CRUMB TOPPING

½ cup light brown sugar

2 tablespoons all-purpose flour

¾ teaspoon cinnamon

½ teaspoon grated fresh ginger

¼ teaspoon nutmeg

¼ teaspoon salt

8 tablespoons (1 stick) unsalted butter, cut
into 8 to 10 small chunks

1¼ cups quick rolled oats

directions

Preheat the oven to 350 degrees. Roll the pie dough into a 12-inch circle. Press into a 9-inch pie plate. Crimp the edges and place in the freezer for 15 minutes to chill.

For the filling, whisk the bourbon, cornstarch, cinnamon, ginger and vanilla in a large bowl. Add the peaches and toss to coat. Sprinkle with the brown sugar and mix well. Pour into the pie shell.

For the crumb topping, combine the brown sugar, flour, cinnamon, ginger, nutmeg and salt in a food processor. Pulse several times to mix. Add the butter and pulse the mixture several times. Add the oats in 3 batches, pulsing a couple of times after each addition until the mixture is crumbly. Top the pie with the crumble.

Bake the pie for 40 to 50 minutes until the crust is cooked through and both the crust and crumb topping are golden brown. Cool the pie on a wire rack.

Makes 8 servings.

Basic Pie Dough

ingredients

2½ cups all-purpose flour

1 teaspoon salt

1 tablespoon sugar

16 tablespoons (2 sticks) frozen unsalted
  butter, cut into cubes

7 tablespoons cold water

directions

Combine the flour, salt and sugar in a food processor fitted with a metal blade. Add the butter and pulse until the mixture resembles coarse meal. Add 1 tablespoon of water at a time, pulsing after each addition. Remove the dough to a work surface. Wrap in plastic wrap and refrigerate for about 1 hour until firm. Roll into desired size.

Makes enough for 2 crusts or 48 mini muffin-size shells.

pie crust vodka trick

For a tender, flaky pie crust, try replacing half of the water with vodka (or other alcohol 80-proof or higher). The vodka allows you to work the dough just as if you had used ice water, but all the alcohol evaporates in the oven, leaving a better-textured crust. There's less gluten formation, so your pie crust will be more tender.

Buttermilk Pie

ingredients

8 tablespoons (1 stick) butter, softened

1½ cups sugar

3 eggs

1 teaspoon vanilla extract

3 tablespoons flour, plus extra for dusting

Pinch of salt

1 cup buttermilk

1 unbaked deep dish pie shell or ½ recipe
  Basic Pie Dough (see above)

directions

Preheat the oven to 400 degrees. Beat the butter and sugar in a bowl with a mixer until light. Beat in the eggs, then the vanilla.

Sift together the flour and salt. Add to the butter mixture alternately with the buttermilk. Beat until smooth.

Pour the filling into the pie shell. Dust lightly with sifted flour. Bake for 10 minutes. Reduce the temperature to 350 degrees. Bake 50 minutes more, or until the pie is golden brown and a knife inserted into the center comes out clean.

Makes 8 servings.

Walnut Pumpkin Pie

A decadent upgrade to the traditional pumpkin pie, and a big hit at Thanksgiving dinner each year.

ingredients

PIE FILLING AND CRUST

1 (15-ounce) can pumpkin purée

1 (14-ounce) can sweetened
   condensed milk

1 large egg

1¼ teaspoons cinnamon

½ teaspoon ground ginger

½ teaspoon nutmeg

¼ teaspoon salt

1 graham cracker pie crust

TOPPING

¼ cup packed light brown sugar

2 to 3 tablespoons cold butter

2 tablespoons all-purpose flour

½ teaspoon cinnamon

¾ cup chopped walnuts

directions

Preheat the oven to 425 degrees.

For the pie filling, combine the pumpkin, sweetened condensed milk, egg, cinnamon, ginger, nutmeg and salt in a bowl and mix well. Pour into the pie crust. Bake for 15 minutes. Remove from the oven. Reduce the temperature to 350 degrees.

For the topping, combine the brown sugar, butter, flour and cinnamon with a pastry blender. Stir in the walnuts to form a crumbly mixture. Sprinkle over the filling. Return to the oven and bake for 40 minutes, or until a knife inserted in the center comes out clean.

Makes 8 servings.

Mystery Pecan Pie

If the usual pecan pie is too sweet for your taste, try this one. The mystery ingredient is cream cheese!

ingredients

PIE CRUST

½ recipe Basic Pie Dough (page 134) or purchased pie shell

FILLING

8 ounces cream cheese, softened

⅓ cup sugar

1 teaspoon salt

1 teaspoon vanilla extract

1 egg, beaten

1¼ cups pecans, whole and pieces

TOPPING

3 eggs, beaten

¼ cup sugar

1 cup corn syrup

1 teaspoon vanilla extract

directions

Preheat the oven to 375 degrees. Fit the pie pastry into a pie dish and refrigerate.

For the pie filling, beat the cream cheese, sugar, salt, vanilla and egg in a bowl until creamy. Pour the cream cheese mixture into the unbaked pie crust. Top with the pecans.

Combine the topping ingredients until well blended. Pour evenly over the pecans. Bake for 30 to 40 minutes, or until firm in the center. Cool completely before cutting.

Makes 8 servings.

Pecan Crust Cheesecake

ingredients

1½ cups graham cracker crumbs or
    gingersnap crumbs

8 tablespoons (1 stick) butter, melted

⅓ cup finely chopped pecans

16 ounces cream cheese, softened

1 cup plus 2 tablespoons sugar, divided

1 cup sour cream

2 teaspoons vanilla extract

Pecan halves for garnish

directions

Preheat the oven to 325 degrees. Combine the graham cracker crumbs, butter and pecans in a bowl and mix well. Press into a 9-inch pie pan.

Beat the cream cheese with 1 cup of the sugar until smooth and creamy. Spoon into the crust and smooth the top. Bake for 20 minutes.

Combine the remaining 2 tablespoons sugar, sour cream and vanilla in a bowl and mix well. Spoon over the partially baked cheesecake. Return to the oven. Increase the temperature to 350 degrees. Bake for 10 minutes longer to form a crackly topping. Garnish with pecan halves. Chill for at least 4 hours before serving.

Makes 10 to 12 servings.

Blueberry Peach Buckle

ingredients

1 cup all-purpose flour

1⅔ cups sugar, divided

½ teaspoon salt

1 tablespoon baking powder

1 teaspoon cinnamon

1 cup milk

8 tablespoons (1 stick) butter

2 cups chopped peaches, thawed and
    drained if frozen

1½ cups blueberries

Vanilla ice cream for serving

directions

Preheat the oven to 350 degrees. Sift together the flour, 1 cup of the sugar, the salt, baking powder and cinnamon. Stir in the milk to form a batter.

Melt the butter in a 9-inch square or 12 x 8-inch glass baking dish. Swirl to coat the bottom of the pan. Pour the batter over the butter, but do not stir. Top with the fruit, but do not mix. Sprinkle with the remaining ⅔ cup sugar. Bake for 1 hour—the batter will rise over the fruit. Serve warm with vanilla ice cream.

Makes 12 servings.

Coconut Cup Custards

The caramel layer on the bottom of these custards will harden as it cools, then melt again as the custard cooks.

ingredients

1¼ cups sugar, divided

1 (15-ounce) can unsweetened coconut milk

¼ cup (about) whole milk or half-and-half

3 eggs

⅛ teaspoon salt

1 teaspoon vanilla extract, dark rum or coconut rum

⅓ to ½ cup shredded unsweetened coconut, toasted, for garnish

directions

Preheat the oven to 350 degrees.

Cook ½ cup of the sugar in a small saucepan over medium-low heat until it melts and browns. Watch carefully—once it begins to brown, it can burn quickly. Divide the caramel among six (½-cup) ramekins or custard cups.

Combine the coconut milk and enough whole milk in a measuring cup to equal 2 cups. Combine with the remaining ¾ cup sugar, the eggs, salt and vanilla. Pour through a strainer 3 times. Pour over the caramel in the ramekins.

Place the ramekins in a large baking dish and pour hot water around the cups. Bake in the water bath for 40 minutes, or until firm. Cool on a rack. Chill, covered, in the refrigerator for at least 2 hours before serving. The custard can be made up to 2 days before serving but tastes best served the day it is made.

To unmold the custards, run a knife around the inside edges of the ramekins, then invert onto small plates. Garnish with toasted coconut.

Makes 6 servings.

traditional cup custards

For more traditional custard, use 2 cups whole milk instead of the coconut/milk mixture; replace the coconut rum with vanilla extract; and omit the coconut garnish. Enjoy!

Chocolate Mousse

This mousse is more complicated than some mousse recipes, but it is worth the effort. The finished product is delicious and stable enough to use for cake filling, or to pipe onto cupcakes, as well as serving on its own.

ingredients

¾ cup heavy cream

1 egg

2 egg yolks

¼ cup sugar

2 tablespoons water

4 ounces 60% cacao bittersweet chocolate

directions

Whip the cream in a mixer until it holds soft peaks. The stiffer the peaks, the stiffer the mousse.

Beat the egg and egg yolks in the bowl of a stand mixer until fluffy.

Combine the sugar and water in a saucepan. Bring to a boil, and cook until the mixture reaches 240 degrees.

Melt the chocolate in a large bowl in the microwave, stirring at 30-second intervals, until melted and very warm.

With the mixer running, pour the hot sugar mixture into the egg mixture by tablespoons, mixing well after each addition to temper the eggs and keep them from scrambling. Quickly stir the egg mixture into the chocolate with a spatula. Fold in the whipped cream.

Spoon the mousse into small ramekins or into a pastry bag. Refrigerate for at least 4 hours. Serve in ramekins or pipe onto dessert plates.

Makes 4 servings.

Meyer Lemon Curd

If you can't find Meyer lemons, substitute ½ cup blend of 3 parts lemon juice to 1 part orange juice.

ingredients

3 or 4 Meyer lemons (about 1 pound)

½ cup sugar

2 large eggs

8 tablespoons (1 stick) butter, cut
   into 4 pieces

directions

Finely grate enough zest from the lemons to measure 2 teaspoons. Squeeze the lemons to obtain ½ cup juice.

Whisk together the zest, juice, sugar and eggs in a metal bowl. Add the butter. Set the bowl over a saucepan of simmering water. Cook, whisking, for about 5 minutes until thickened and smooth. (An instant-read thermometer should read about 160 degrees.)

Force the curd through a fine sieve set over another bowl. Serve warm or cover the surface of the curd with wax paper or plastic wrap cut to fit, and cool completely.

Makes about 1⅔ cups.

COOKIES & CANDIES

WEST SIDE SQUARES

By agreement between Oglethorpe and Chief Tomo-chi-chi, the area west of Jefferson Street belonged to the Yamacraw Indians. After the Revolutionary War, the Indians were forced westward as the city expanded. The "West End" became known as the aristocratic quarter of the city, where Savannah's wealthiest families lived in mansions with elaborate gardens and grounds. Horse cars were replaced by streetcars and jitneys by buses, then both replaced by cars, and gradually the automobile's encroachments curved the edges of our squares and transformed Savannah's western neighborhoods. Only a few of the original homes still stand in the squares that were developed around them in the impingement of the expanding city.

FRANKLIN SQUARE, FRANKLIN WARD —1790

Franklin Square was designed in 1790 and named to honor Benjamin Franklin, Georgia's agent in her affairs with Great Britain, and also the contributor of seeds for upland rice and the Chinese tallow (popcorn) tree. The square was called the Water Tank or Reservoir Square because the distributing reservoir was sited there in 1854. In 1935, Franklin Square was divided into east and west segments when Montgomery Street bisected it, to conform to federal highway regulations. The square was Savannah's first square to be reclaimed in 1985.

In 2012, a monument commemorating the Haitian involvement in the Siege of Savannah was constructed. The first African Baptist Church of Savannah, the nation's oldest African-American congregation, was founded here in 1788 on a lot purchased by African Americans from Andrew Bryan. Originally known as the "Brick Church", the building features the original pipe organ, baptismal pool, pews, and a false floor with African designs symbolizing safety, under which slaves hid during their Underground Railroad journey to freedom.

ORLEANS SQUARE, JACKSON WARD —1815

Jackson Ward and Orleans Square were established by the city in 1815 to pay tribute to General Andrew Jackson, hero of the battle of New Orleans (War of 1812) and future president of the United States. Orleans Square was once surrounded by outstanding and prestigious homes, including the Champion-Fowlkes House and buildings along the southeast tithing block. Construction of the City Auditorium in 1916 compromised the western trust lots and forced the demolition of William Jay's 1818, Bulloch-Habersham House. Urban renewal further destroyed the ward when the City Auditorium, its grounds, and the surrounding tithing

opposite page: *Gorgeous landscape can be found in Chatham Square.*

buildings were razed for the construction of the 1971 Civic Center. Luckily, the square itself remained intact; the same federal urban renewal funding that destroyed the ward was later spent on beautifying this square and five others. The Junior League of Savannah contributed $3,000 towards the consulting services of Carl Feiss, F.A.I.A., who recommended an architectural inventory of Savannah to stem the demolition of the city's historic structures erected between 1733 to 1856. The 1958 survey, conducted through a collaboration with the Historic Savannah Foundation, was included in the first edition of Historic Savannah, towards which the League contributed $10,000 for its publication. In addition, the League subsidized the hiring of Historic Savannah Foundation's first executive director, and League members served on the executive and steering committees.

PULASKI SQUARE, PULASKI WARD —1837

Built in a time of patriotic prosperity, Pulaski Square was laid out in 1837 along with Lafayette and Madison Squares, all of which pay tribute to Revolutionary War heroes. Benjamin Franklin befriended Count Casimir Pulaski in Paris, and enticed the Count to join the fight for American independence. He served the Continental Army as founder of the American Cavalry, "Commander of the Horse", from 1777 until his death during the Siege of Savannah in 1779. Southwest of Savannah at the Spring Hill Redoubt, a cannon's grapeshot fatally struck the general as he attempted to break through British lines.

Pulaski Square's landscape once displayed long diagonal bands of azalea bushes that resembled the Confederate Flag's St. Andrew's Cross. This design honored Confederate War hero General Francis Bartow, whose home and porch overlook the square from the east corner of Harris and Barnard Streets. In partnership with the Historic Savannah Foundation (HSF), Junior League members participated in the Pulaski Square/West Jones Street area redevelopment project, which successfully launched HSF's Revolving Loan program.

CHATHAM SQUARE, CHATHAM WARD —1847

By the time the final four squares were laid out in the 1840s and 1850s, the final four Savannah squares exhausted the last of the common property that Oglethorpe reserved for the colony. Chatham was the last ward developed from the Western Common. Chatham Ward and Square were named for William Pitt, prime minister of Great Britain and First Earl of Chatham during the eighteenth century. Limited land resulted in truncating the western portion of the ward plan. Both the trust and tithing lots are much smaller than the eastern lots.

Chatham Ward was the slated site of the first school in the city (Massie School); however, because of the remote location, Massie School was relocated and on that site is one of the last downtown school buildings - Barnard Street School (1906), which is now owned by the Savannah College of Art & Design. Chatham Square was a playground for school children, a public land use controversy that lasted almost eighty years.

Savannah's historically significant architecture provides each square a backdrop. Nowhere can this be seen better then looking at Gordon Row on the southeast tithing block. An entire uninterrupted block, Gordon Row is made up of 15 identical four story houses sharing common side walls. Demolition of a historic building or the construction of incompatible infill on any one of Oglethorpe's lots greatly affects the distinctive grace of Savannah's squares.

Brown Butter Cream Cheese Chocolate Chip Cookies

Using a ½-inch to 1-inch scoop of dough and slightly flattening the cookies before baking produces big, bakery-style cookies that are pretty much impossible to resist!

ingredients

16 tablespoons (2 sticks) butter

4 ounces cream cheese, softened

¾ cup brown sugar

¾ cup granulated sugar

2 eggs

2 teaspoons vanilla extract

3¼ cups all-purpose flour, sifted

1 teaspoon salt

1 teaspoon baking soda

2 cups chocolate chips

directions

Melt the butter in a saucepan and heat until it is browned. Let cool. Beat the melted butter with the cream cheese, brown sugar and granulated sugar with an electric mixer in a bowl until smooth. Add the eggs and vanilla and beat to combine.

Turn the mixer to low and beat in the flour, salt and baking soda just until combined. Add the chocolate chips and mix just until incorporated. Refrigerate the dough, covered, for several hours until chilled.

When ready to bake, preheat the oven to 375 degrees. Line 2 or 3 baking sheets with parchment paper. Use an ice cream scoop to portion out 2-inch (approximately 1/4 cup) balls of dough and arrange on the baking sheets. Flatten slightly. Bake for 9 to 12 minutes, or until the edges are golden.

Makes 2 dozen large cookies.

brown butter

Brown butter is just regular butter than has been heated until it browns. It smells like hazelnuts and has a similar nutty color. When your butter is a shade lighter than you think it should be, give it a final stir or swirl, turn off your heat and pour the butter into a heatproof container. Butter will continue to brown when you take if off the heat. Watch closely, as perfect brown butter can turn into burnt butter in seconds.

Triple Chocolate Chip Cookies

ingredients

1 (24-ounce) package semisweet chocolate chips

16 tablespoons (2 sticks) butter, softened

1 cup packed light brown sugar

1 teaspoon vanilla extract

2 large eggs

2½ cups all-purpose flour

1½ teaspoons baking soda

½ teaspoon salt

1 (4- to 6-ounce) bar white chocolate, cut into small chunks

directions

Melt 1½ cups of the chips in a saucepan over low heat, stirring constantly. Let cool to room temperature, but not firm up.

Preheat the oven to 350 degrees. Beat the butter, brown sugar and vanilla in a bowl with a mixer until fluffy. Add the eggs, one at a time, beating well after each addition. Beat in the melted chocolate until the mixture is fluffy. Beat in the flour, baking soda and salt. Stir in the remaining chocolate chips and the white chocolate chunks.

Arrange small scoops of the dough on ungreased baking sheets. Bake for 12 to 15 minutes. Cool completely on a wire rack.

Makes 50 large or 75 small cookies.

Chocolate Chip Oat "Meal" Cookies

These are soft but substantial chocolate chip cookies that stay soft.

ingredients

2½ cups old-fashioned oats

1 cup packed dark brown sugar

1 cup granulated sugar

16 tablespoons (2 sticks) butter, softened

2 eggs

1½ teaspoons vanilla extract

2 cups all-purpose flour (can use up to
    1 cup whole wheat flour)

1 tablespoon baking powder

1 teaspoon salt

12 ounces dark chocolate chips

directions

Grind the oats into flour in batches in a blender or food processor.

Beat the brown sugar, granulated sugar and butter in a large mixing bowl. Beat the eggs and vanilla lightly in a small bowl. Add to the mixer, beating just until blended.

Add the flour, baking powder and salt to the ground oats and mix with a spoon to blend. Add to the butter mixture in batches until incorporated. Stir in the chocolate chips until evenly distributed.

Chill the dough for 30 to 45 minutes. (Chilling it less will result in sticky dough; chilling it more will result in dough that is too firm.)

Preheat the oven to 350 degrees. Line 2 or 3 baking sheets with parchment paper. Form the dough into balls or drop by teaspoonsfuls or tablespoonfuls onto the baking sheets. Bake for 9 to 11 minutes. Let the cookies cool on waxed paper on the counter to keep them soft and chewy. Store the cooled cookies in an airtight container. .

Note: The dough can be formed into balls and frozen on a cookie sheet. Once frozen, transfer to a heavy-duty ziptop bag or storage container and freeze until ready to bake. You can bake them directly from the freezer for 11 to 13 minutes.

Makes 38 to 60 cookies.

Cranberry Walnut Oatmeal Cookies with Variations

ingredients

12 tablespoons (1½ **sticks**)
  butter, softened

1 cup packed brown sugar

½ cup granulated sugar

1 egg

¼ cup water

1 teaspoon vanilla extract

3 cups uncooked old-fashioned oats

1 cup all-purpose flour

1 teaspoon salt

½ teaspoon baking soda

1 cup dried cranberries

1 cup chopped walnuts

directions

Preheat the oven to 350 degrees. Line baking sheets with parchment paper.

Beat the butter, brown sugar and granulated sugar in a bowl until light and fluffy. Beat in the egg, water and vanilla until creamy. Combine the oats, flour, salt and baking soda in a bowl. Add to the butter mixture in batches, mixing well after each addition. Fold in the cranberries and walnuts just until combined.

Drop the dough by rounded teaspoonfuls onto the baking sheets. Bake for 15 to 20 minutes.

Variations: You can change up the flavors in this flexible recipe. Let your taste buds be your guide!

White Chocolate–Coconut Oatmeal Cookies: Substitute 12 ounces milk chocolate chips and ½ cup flaked coconut for the cranberries and walnuts. Or, if you prefer, add them in addition to the cranberries and walnuts, or use any combination of the ingredients that you like.

Soft Oatmeal Raisin Cookies: Omit the dried cranberries. Simmer ¾ cup raisins in ¼ cup water for about 5 minutes. Drain, reserving raisin liquid, and allow raisins to cool. Use ¼ cup of the reserved raisin liquid in place of the water called for in the recipe. (Add water if needed to reach ¼ cup.) Add the raisins with the walnuts, if desired. The moist raisins and raisin water make for outstanding flavor and moist, chewy cookies.

Makes about 60 cookies.

Wedding Tea Cakes (Mexican Wedding Cookies)

ingredients

16 tablespoons (2 sticks) butter, softened

½ cup confectioners' sugar,
    plus extra for coating cookies

1 teaspoon almond extract

2¼ cups sifted all-purpose flour

¼ teaspoon salt

¾ cup finely chopped pecans

directions

Preheat the oven to 400 degrees. Line 2 or 3 baking sheets with parchment paper.

Beat the butter and confectioners' sugar until creamy. Add the almond extract, flour, salt and pecans and mix well. Form the mixture into nickel-sized balls (or flatten if preferred). Arrange on the baking sheets. Bake for 12 to 15 minutes. Let cool for a few minutes, and then roll the warm cookies in confectioners' sugar. Let cool completely, and then roll again in confectioners' sugar.

Makes 48 to 72 cookies.

Molasses Spice Cookies

ingredients

1 cup sugar, plus extra for rolling

8 tablespoons (1 stick) butter, softened

¼ cup shortening

1 egg

¼ cup molasses

2 to 2½ cups all-purpose flour

½ teaspoon salt

2 teaspoons baking powder

½ teaspoon ground cloves

½ teaspoon ground ginger

1 teaspoon cinnamon

directions

Preheat the oven to 350 degrees. Beat the sugar, butter and shortening in a bowl until creamy. Add the egg and molasses and mix well. Combine the flour, salt, baking powder, cloves, ginger and cinnamon in another bowl and mix well. Add to the butter mixture gradually, beating until well combined.

Roll the dough into 1-inch balls. Roll in sugar to coat. Arrange on a baking sheet and bake for 8 to 10 minutes until the tops begin cracking.

Note: To measure molasses or other sticky ingredients cleanly, spray the measuring cup with nonstick cooking spray before pouring in the molasses.

Makes 36 cookies.

Strawberry Lemonade Bars

ingredients

CRUST

¼ cup sugar

8 tablespoons (1 stick) butter, softened

1½ cups all-purpose flour

¼ teaspoon salt

FILLING

2 to 3 teaspoons grated lemon zest

1 cup fresh lemon juice

½ cup puréed strawberries
(about ¾ cup strawberries)

1¼ cups granulated sugar

4 large eggs

¼ cup all-purpose flour

½ teaspoon baking powder

¼ teaspoon salt

Confectioners' sugar, for dusting

directions

Preheat oven to 350 degrees. Lightly grease a 13 x 9-inch baking pan

For the crust, beat the sugar and butter in a bowl until smooth and fluffy. Beat in the flour and salt gradually until the mixture is crumbly. Press into the bottom of the prepared baking in an even layer. Bake for 17 minutes, or until set at the edges.

For the filling, combine the lemon zest, lemon juice, strawberry purée, granulated sugar and eggs in a food processor. Pulse to blend until smooth. Add the flour, baking powder and salt and pulse until smooth.

Pour the filling carefully over the hot crust. Return to the oven for 22 to 26 minutes, until the filling is set. There will be a light colored "crust" on top from the sugar in the custard.

Cool completely. Use a damp knife to cut into bars to ensure clean slices. Store the bars in the refrigerator, and sprinkle with confectioners' sugar before serving.

Makes 24 bars.

Carmelitas

ingredients

32 caramel squares, unwrapped

½ cup heavy cream

12 tablespoons (1½ sticks) butter, melted

¾ cup packed brown sugar

1 cup all-purpose flour

1 cup rolled oats

1 teaspoon baking soda

6 ounces semisweet chocolate chips

directions

Preheat the oven to 350 degrees. Combine the caramels and cream in a small saucepan over low heat (or in the top of a double boiler over simmering water). Heat, stirring frequently, until completely melted and smooth.

Combine the butter, brown sugar, flour, oats and baking soda in a bowl. Press half of the oatmeal mixture evenly into the bottom of an 8-inch square baking pan. Bake for 10 minutes. Remove from the oven and sprinkle the chocolate chips over the crust. Pour the caramel mixture over the chocolate chips. Crumble the remaining oatmeal mixture over the caramel.

Return to the oven and bake for 15 to 20 minutes longer, or until the edges are lightly browned. Cool completely before cutting. Store and serve at room temperature.

Makes 20 to 24 cookies.

carmelita variations

For variations, add 1 cup chopped pecans and/or 1 cup unsweetened shredded coconut over the chocolate chips. A stint in the fridge will help the carmelitas to cool off if you are pinched for time. They should not be served cold, but molten caramel takes a long time to cool down. To make a 13 x 9-inch version, double the recipe and cook 5 to 10 additional minutes after the last addition of the caramel.

Pecan Tassies

ingredients

1 recipe Basic Pie Dough (page 134)

2 eggs

1½ cups packed light brown sugar

4 tablespoons (½ stick) butter, melted

1⅓ cups pecan pieces, chopped

1 teaspoon vanilla extract

directions

Preheat the oven to 325 degrees. Divide the dough into four portions. Divide each portion into 12 pieces. Roll each piece into balls. Press each dough ball into a cup in an ungreased mini muffin pan, covering the bottom and sides to form a pie crust.

Combine the eggs, brown sugar, butter, pecans and vanilla in a bowl and mix well. Spoon evenly into the prepared mini pie shells. Bake for 25 minutes, or until edges are browned.

Makes 48 tassies.

Date Nut Balls

ingredients

8 ounces chopped dates

8 tablespoons (1 stick) butter or margarine

½ cup brown sugar

½ cup granulated sugar

2 cups puffed white rice cereal

2 cups chopped pecans

Confectioners' sugar for rolling

directions

Combine the dates, butter, brown sugar and granulated sugar in a large saucepan. Cook over low heat for at least 5 minutes, or until the margarine is melted. Remove from the heat and stir in the cereal and pecans.

Shape the mixture into small balls. Roll in confectioners' sugar while warm.

Makes about 60 pieces.

Southern Toffee

ingredients

½ cup pecan pieces

12 ounces (3 sticks) butter, wrappers saved

1½ cups sugar

4 (15-ounce) milk chocolate bars,
  broken into pieces

directions

Preheat the oven to 350 degrees. Toast the pecans on a baking sheet for 10 minutes, taking care not to let them burn.

Use the butter wrappers to butter a rimmed baking sheet.

Combine the butter and sugar in a deep 3-quart pot over medium heat. (Do not use nonstick.) Put a candy thermometer in the pot. Heat until the butter melts, stirring occasionally with a silicone spatula or wooden spoon. Cook, stirring constantly, until the mixture reaches 290 degrees on a candy thermometer (the soft crack stage). Do not overcook or the butter will separate. Pour the mixture immediately onto the baking sheet.

Let cool for a few minutes. Top with the pieces of chocolate bar. When the chocolate is soft and glossy, use an offset spatula to spread into an even layer. Sprinkle immediately with pecans, patting them into the soft chocolate. Let cool completely—a cold porch or refrigerator will speed up the process.

Use the back side of a knife or an offset spatula to crack the toffee into pieces about 2x2 inches.

Makes 26 to 48 pieces.

Grandma's Peanut Brittle

ingredients

2 cups sugar

1 cup light corn syrup

½ cup water

1 cup (2 sticks) butter or margarine

2 cups raw Spanish peanuts

2 tablespoons baking soda

directions

Grease 2 baking sheets with butter. Combine the sugar, corn syrup and water in a large, heavy saucepan. Cook, stirring constantly, over medium heat until the sugar dissolves. Bring to a boil and then add the butter. Using a candy thermometer, cook until the mixture reaches 230 degrees, and then continue to cook, stirring frequently, until the temperature reaches 280 degrees. Add the peanuts and cook, stirring constantly, until the mixture reaches 305 degrees (hard crack stage).

Quickly stir in the baking soda and then pour the mixture onto the prepared baking sheets. Cool to room temperature. Break into pieces and store in an airtight container or heavy-duty ziptop plastic bag.

Makes 36 to 48 pieces.

Georgia's Gorgeous Peanut Butter Gems

ingredients

2 cups (12 ounces) chocolate chips or semisweet chocolate pieces

2 cups crunchy peanut butter

1½ cups graham cracker crumbs

16 tablespoons (2 sticks) butter, melted

3 cups (about ¾ pound) confectioners' sugar

directions

Melt the chocolate chips in the microwave or in the top of a double boiler set over simmering water.

Combine the peanut butter, graham cracker crumbs, butter and confectioners' sugar in another bowl. Press into the bottom of a 13 x 9-inch pan. Spread the melted chocolate over the top. Chill until firm. Cut into small squares.

Note: This recipe doubles well, and these bars freeze well. Separate layers of bars with a sheet of waxed paper.

Makes 24 squares.

Ellis Square was one of the four lost squares that was reclaimed in 2010.

BEVERAGES, SAUCES, & CONDIMENTS

LOST SQUARES

Development in the twentieth century resulted in the destruction of the Montgomery Street Squares, as they were bisected for U.S. Highway 17 traffic in 1935, leaving only their landscaped eastern and western sections. During the 1960s and 1970s, the city saw the construction of the Savannah Civic Center and the Chatham County Complex on Montgomery Street. Residential neighborhoods were sacrificed for the buildings and their parking structures, eliminating their adjoining squares, the historic building stock, and the tree-lined streets and lanes.

LIBERTY SQUARE, LIBERTY WARD —1799

Liberty Square was established in 1799 to "perpetuate the dawn of freedom and independence" in honor of the Sons of Liberty, in whom the roots of the American Revolution lay. While much of Georgia remained loyalist through the early independence movement, a Savannah group known as the Liberty Boys met regularly at Tondee's Tavern for political discussions. The group included men of Savannah's most notable families—Telfair, Habersham, John Houston, Noble Wymberly Jones, and others—and was responsible for incidents of sabotage, demonstrations of disloyalty to the Crown (including the tarring and feathering of a loyalist), and seizure of gunpowder from the British.

Liberty Square's last remaining historic residences and commercial buildings can be seen in York Street tithing block and along Jefferson Street. Originally laid in what remained of Elbert Square on the fiftieth anniversary of the American Legion, the soaring Flame of Freedom was re-erected on the remains of Liberty Square in front of the new courthouse in 1985.

ELBERT SQUARE, ELBERT WARD —1801

After the devastating fire of 1796, the city enacted the construction of cisterns and wells in its squares. To pay for these improvements, Elbert Ward and Square were established in 1801 and marketed as worthy residential sites. The Honorable Samuel Elbert was one of Savannah's most illustrious citizens—a brilliant soldier and leader in the Revolutionary War, sheriff of Chatham County, and governor of Georgia before his premature death at 48. Originally laid to rest in an undisclosed location on his family's land, Elbert's remains were uncovered on an Indian mound overlooking the Savannah River in 1971 and reinterred with full military honors in Colonial Park.

Wars, the Great Depression, and the development of rail facilities on the west side of town took a toll on Elbert Ward, which declined and became a tenement district. After construction of the Civic Center, a sliver of Elbert Square remains as a small green space.

Bourbon Slush

Remember that this drink will only be as good as the bourbon you use, so choose a good-quality bourbon. Make the drink weaker or stronger by adjusting the quantity of bourbon. Bourbon Slush is good in any type of glass, but an old-fashioned glass is typical.

ingredients

3 tea bags

2 cups boiling water

1½ cups sugar

1 (6-ounce) can frozen orange juice concentrate, thawed

1 (12-ounce) can frozen citrus or lemonade concentrate, thawed

2 cups water

2 to 3 cups bourbon whiskey

Ginger ale or lemon-lime soda, chilled

directions

Steep the tea bags in the boiling water for 30 minutes. Combine the tea, sugar, orange juice concentrate, lemonade concentrate, water and whiskey in a large freezer bag or freezer-safe container. Freeze for 8 to 48 hours. (The bourbon will prevent the mixture from freezing solid.)

For each serving, scoop enough slush mixture to fill a glass three-fourths full. Top with chilled ginger ale or lemon-lime soda. Don't stir—just let the soda blend with the slush mixture before drinking.

Makes 8 to 10 servings.

Rosemary-Infused Watermelon Lemonade

This summer drink can be served in a Collins glass or in a sugar-rimmed martini glass garnished with a small watermelon wedge, a lemon twist and a sprig of rosemary.

ingredients

2 cups water

1 cup sugar

¼ cup fresh rosemary
   needles, chopped

2 cups lemon juice, divided

12 cups cubed seedless
   watermelon, divided

2 tablespoons honey

directions

Make a simple syrup by bringing the water and sugar to a boil in a small saucepan. Add the rosemary and remove from the heat. Steep, covered, for at least 2 hours.

Combine 1 cup of the lemon juice and 6 cups of the watermelon in a blender or food processor. Strain rosemary simple syrup through a mesh strainer into the blender. Cover and purée until smooth. Strain the purée through a mesh strainer into a pitcher, and discard the solids Purée the remaining lemon juice, watermelon and the honey in the blender, then strain into the pitcher. Stir to combine well. Chill. Serve over ice.

Note: This lemonade is delicious as a summer cocktail when combined with vodka and orange liqueur such as Triple Sec. Use equal parts vodka and Triple Sec to 8 parts lemonade.

Makes 6 to 8 servings.

Mary's Knees

A tasty and different brunch cocktail.

ingredients

Juice of 12 oranges, or 1/2 (12-ounce)
    can orange juice concentrate plus
    3 cups water

1¼ cups vodka

½ cup orange liqueur such as Cointreau

¼ cup Campari

Juice of 2 limes

directions

Combine all the ingredients in a 2-quart pitcher. Mix well. Chill for 3 hours or until very cold. Add ice cubes to the pitcher. Serve the drinks in stemmed 8-ounce glasses.

Makes 6 (8-ounce) servings.

Coffee Punch with a Punch

ingredients

1 pint (2 cups) milk

8 cups strong coffee, cooled

2 teaspoons vanilla extract

⅓ cup sugar

1 cup (½ pint) heavy whipping cream

1 quart vanilla ice cream, softened

Ground nutmeg

40 ounces coffee liqueur or
    chocolate liqueur

directions

Combine the milk, coffee, vanilla and sugar in a bowl and mix well. Beat the whipping cream in a stand mixer until soft peaks form.

Spoon the softened ice cream into a punch bowl. Pour in the coffee mixture. Top with the whipped cream. Dust with nutmeg.

To serve, pour 2 ounces of the coffee or chocolate liqueur into a glass. Top with the coffee punch. For any tee-totalers, simply skip the liqueur. It's still delicious!

Makes 18 to 20 servings.

Chatham Artillery Punch

ingredients

2 gallons green tea
    (1 pound loose tea steeped for
    several hours in 2 gallons water)

Juice of 36 lemons

5 pounds brown sugar

2 gallons Catawba wine

2 gallons Santa Cruz rum

1 gallon Hennessy (3 star) brandy

1 gallon dry gin

1 gallon rye whiskey

2 quarts maraschino cherries, drained

2 quarts pineapple cubes, drained

10 quarts Champagne

directions

Mix the tea and lemon juice in a container large enough to hold 13 gallons, preferably in a cedar tub. Add the brown sugar, wine, rum, brandy, gin and whiskey. Let this mixture stand, covered, for at least one week, preferably two. It should not be refrigerated.

When ready to serve, pour over a large slab of ice in a punch bowl. (Do not use crushed ice or ice cubes.) Add the cherries, pineapple and Champagne, pouring in slowly and mixing with a circular motion.

Makes 200 servings.

Quick Marchand de Vin

A traditional Marchand de Vin takes hours and multiple steps that are too hard for many to consider when juggling multiple dishes. This sauce tastes richer and slower to make than it is, which makes it a great accompaniment to beef tenderloin and the ultimate make-ahead dinner party trick.

ingredients

2 tablespoons butter

1½ cups finely chopped green onions

2 teaspoons finely chopped garlic

2 tablespoons all-purpose flour

2 cups beef stock or veal stock,
   plus more if needed for thinning

½ cup finely chopped fresh mushrooms
   (about 4 ounces)

½ cup dry red wine

3 tablespoons lemon juice

1 tablespoon Worcestershire sauce

Scant ⅛ teaspoon cayenne pepper

Scant ⅛ teaspoon white pepper

½ teaspoon salt

directions

Melt the butter in a heavy 1- to 1½-quart saucepan over medium heat. When the foam begins to subside, add the green onions and garlic. Sauté for 5 minutes or until tender but not brown. Add the flour and mix well. Cook briefly.

Add the stock in a thin stream, whisking constantly. Cook over high heat until the sauce boils and thickens, whisking until smooth.

Stir in the mushrooms. Reduce the heat to low and simmer, partially covered, for about 15 to 25 minutes, or until the liquid is reduced by one-third and the mushrooms are tender. Stir in the wine, lemon juice, Worcestershire, cayenne pepper, white pepper and salt. Cook, uncovered, for 10 to 12 minutes over medium heat until thickened. Remove from the heat or hold at very low temperature. Before serving, bring to a simmer and adjust the seasoning and thickness with additional stock, if desired.

Note: For a smooth sauce, blend with an immersion blender.

Makes 2 to 3 cups of sauce.

Almond Cherry Jam

ingredients

5 cups dark sweet cherries, pitted or
    5 cups frozen sweet cherries, thawed

2 (1.75-ounce) packets powdered pectin

3 cups sugar (only 1½ cups sugar if using
    frozen cherries)

1½ teaspoons almond extract

directions

Combine the cherries and pectin in a 4- to 6-quart Dutch oven or saucepan. Cook, stirring, until the pectin dissolves. Add the sugar. Cook, stirring constantly, until the mixture boils. Boil for 4 minutes, stirring constantly. Remove from the heat. Add the almond extract.

Pour the jam into sterilized jars. Wipe the threads and rims clean. Seal the jars. Process for 10 minutes in boiling water to cover by 2 inches.

After opening, store the jam in the refrigerator and use within 2 weeks.

Makes about 4 pints or 8 half-pints.

Watermelon Barbecue Sauce

This unique blend of Georgia favorites is great on chicken, pork, ribs—almost anything on the summer grill.

ingredients

2 cups cubed, seeded watermelon

2 Vidalia onions, coarsely chopped

½ cup ketchup

3 tablespoons apple cider vinegar

3 tablespoons Worcestershire sauce

2 teaspoons honey

1 teaspoon garlic powder

1 teaspoon black pepper

½ teaspoon salt, or to taste

Cayenne pepper to taste

directions

Combine the watermelon, onions, ketchup, vinegar, Worcestershire and honey in a blender. Process to a fine purée.

Pour the purée into a saucepan. Bring to a boil, and then cook until reduced by about 10 percent. Remove from the heat and let cool. Add the garlic powder, black pepper, salt and cayenne pepper. Refrigerate until ready to use.

Makes 2 to 3 cups.

Mayonnaise

Delicious in sandwiches, in salads and over sliced summer tomatoes. Homemade mayonnaise is truly a different food than the store-bought variety.

ingredients

1 whole egg

1 egg yolk

½ teaspoon dry mustard, divided

1 to 2 tablespoons lemon juice, divided

¼ teaspoon salt, or to taste

¼ teaspoon cayenne pepper

¾ to 1 cup vegetable oil

directions

Beat the whole egg until very thoroughly combined in a small bowl. Let it settle, then measure 2 tablespoons of it into a blender or food processor. Add the yolk and ¼ teaspoon of the mustard and process for 5 seconds for a food processor or 15 to 25 seconds for a blender. Scrape down the side of the container, and add 1 tablespoon of the lemon juice, the salt and cayenne pepper. Process for 10 to 15 seconds in a food processor, 1 to 2 minutes in a blender. Drizzle in ¼ cup of the oil in the thinnest stream you can manage. Add the next ½ cup in a slow, steady stream. Stop and scrape down the bowl.

Adjust the consistency by adding up to ¼ cup additional oil to thicken. Season to taste wtih the remaining lemon juice, dry mustard and salt.

Makes about 1 cup.

Blender Hollandaise Sauce

ingredients

10 tablespoons unsalted butter,
   cut into pieces

3 egg yolks

1 tablespoon lemon juice

½ teaspoon salt

⅛ teaspoon cayenne pepper

directions

Melt the butter in a small saucepan; remove from the heat. Combine the egg yolks, lemon juice, salt and cayenne pepper in a blender container. Blend for 20 to 30 seconds until the mixture is lighter in color. Lower the speed and drizzle in the melted butter. Pulse for 10 seconds longer. Adjust the consistency if needed with additional warm butter or water. Taste and adjust the seasonings. Hold for up to 30 to 45 minutes in a warm place near the stove.

Makes ¾ cup.

Mexican Chipotle Seasoning

This seasoning shines on pork, chicken and summer squash or zucchini. For a really easy dip, add to an equal mixture of sour cream and mayonnaise.

ingredients

1 teaspoon ground chipotle pepper, or to taste

½ teaspoon garlic powder or onion powder

½ teaspoon cumin

½ teaspoon cayenne pepper, or to taste

¼ teaspoon salt, or to taste

directions

Combine all the ingredients in a bowl and mix well. Adjust the flavor with cayenne pepper and salt.

Makes about 1 tablespoon.

Taco Seasoning

ingredients

1 tablespoon chili powder

¼ teaspoon garlic powder

¼ teaspoon onion powder

¼ teaspoon red pepper flakes

¼ teaspoon dried oregano

½ teaspoon paprika

1½ teaspoons ground cumin

1 teaspoon sea salt

directions

Combine all of the ingredients in a small bowl and mix well. Store in an airtight container.

Makes about 2 tablespoons.

PARKS

SAVANNAH'S DOWNTOWN PARKS ARE AS BELOVED AS ITS DOWNTOWN SQUARES.

COLONIAL PARK CEMETERY

Established in 1750 and twenty years after the colony was founded, Christ Church Cemetery was the resting place of Savannah's founding citizens. As Savannah expanded, so did the need for a public burial ground. The six-acre cemetery is home to over 9,000 "residents" including patriots of the Revolutionary and Spanish-American Wars, a signer of the Declaration of Independence (Button Gwinnett), Savannah's religious leaders, merchants, politicians, and those who laid the foundation of the colony and commonwealth. There is also at least one "permanent visitor" to the city: Edward Green Malbone, the famous miniaturist painter from New England, visited Savannah and never left. Known as Old Brick Cemetery, it was closed in 1861 and later used as a stabling ground during Savannah's occupation, during which the cemetery suffered further when soldiers defaced the tombstones. In 1896 the city laid out tabby walks, planted trees and flowers to convert the old burying ground into the picturesque Colonial Park Cemetery. New cemeteries at Laurel Grove (1852) and Bonaventure (1869), were designed with elegant promenades between exquisite memorial statuary.

FORSYTH PARK

Savannah's largest downtown park, Forsyth Park, ended the ward and square system of Oglethorpe's exalted city plan begun in 1733. The park, dedicated in 1851, is named for statesman John Forsyth--minister to Spain, congressman, governor of Georgia—who donated the land to increase the park to 30 acres running from Gaston Street at its northern boundary to Park Avenue at its southern end. During the Revolutionary War, the site lay beyond the city's southern boundary and was used as camp for the American and French armies in the Siege of Savannah. A decidedly more peaceful spot now, the park includes gardens, a pavilion, a café, walking, and running paths, tennis and basketball courts and open fields that are enjoyed by hundreds of locals and tourists each day.

The original plan of the park was laid out by William Bischoff but redesigned by John B. Hogg. In the center, a bronze Confederate soldier guards from atop the city's highest monument. City fathers paid extra for its transport route after the monument was cast in Canada: special orders were given that no piece was to touch Yankee ground. Within the cast-iron enclosure are memorial busts of two Confederate heroes, General Lafayette McLaws and Brigadier General Francis S.

opposite page: Pleasure grounds filled with majestic shade trees, green turfs, and paths lead to the Forsyth Park Fountain.

Bartow. A monument dedicated to Spanish-American War veterans lies at the southern terminus of Forsyth Park, where a uniformed soldier of the war faces south toward its enemies. The South had no army at the time, so a militia calling itself the Irish Jasper Greens formed up and went off to fight as the only Savannah regiment represented in the conflict.

The large white fountain in the park, modeled after the fountain in the Place de la Concorde in Paris, has become an iconic image of the city. The water in city fountains is dyed green each year in celebration of St. Patrick's Day; the so-called Greening of the Fountain ceremony in Forsyth Park has become a celebration in itself.

Near its northwest section, the Fragrant Garden is a walled section of the park built in 1959 and landscaped with scented plants in a variety of textures for the visually impaired and all others to enjoy. The park fell into disrepair in the 1970s and 1980s and was closed until its revitalization through the work of the Trustees' Garden Club, the Junior League of Savannah, and the City of Savannah's Park and Tree Department. The park's popularity for recreation and civic events echoes the motto of the Georgia Trustees: Non sibi sed aliis, or "Not for ourselves, but for others."

WORKS CITED

Chatham Savannah Public Library - Vertical File Collection. Print.

Georgia Historical Society - Vertical File Collection. Print.

Hardee, Charles Seton Henry. *Reminiscences and Recollections of Old Savannah*. Publisher Not Identified, 1928. Print.

Harden, William. *A History of Savannah and South Georgia*. Chicago: Lewis Pub., 1913. Print.

Historic Savannah. Savannah, GA: Historic Savannah Foundation, 1968. Print.

Jones, Charles C., O. F. Vedder, and Frank Weldon. *History of Savannah, Ga.; From Its Settlement to the Close of the Eighteenth Century*. Syracuse, NY: D. Mason, 1890. Print.

Lane, Mills. *Savannah Revisited: A Pictorial History*. Savannah, GA: Beehive, 1973. Print.

Olmstead, Charles H. *Art Work of Savannah*. Chicago: W.H. Parish Pub., 1893. Print.

Savannah Chatham Public Library - Georgia Collection. Print.

Savannah Morning News archives. *Savannahnow.com*. n.p. Web. 21 Oct. 2014.

Savannah. Savannah, GA: Review Print., 1937. Print.

"Savannah Squares." *Visit-Historic-Savannah.com*. n.p. Web. 2014. <http://www.visit-historic-savannah.com/savannah-squares.html>.

Sieg, Edward Chan. *The Squares: An Introduction to Savannah*. Norfolk: Donning, 1984. Print.

"Squares and Parks." *VisitSavannah.com*. n.p. Web. 2014 <http://www.visitsavannah.com/essential-savannah/squares-parks.aspx>.

"Squares of Savannah, Georgia." *Wikipedia*. Wikimedia Foundation. Web. 27 Feb. 2015. <http://en.wikipedia.org/wiki/Squares_of_Savannah,_Georgia>.

This Guide to the City of Savannah. Savannah: Junior League of Savannah, 1946. Print.

Toledano, Roulhac. *The National Trust Guide to Savannah*. New York: Preservation, 1997. Print.

Wilson, Adelaide, and Georgia Weymouth. *Historic and Picturesque Savannah*. Boston: Published for the Subscribers by the Boston Photogravure, 1889. Print.

INDEX

CONTRIBUTORS

Emma Adler
Marcie Adler
Tara Aikens
Sarah Aliffi-Baez
Shay Ayer
Brianne Baggett
Melissa Beaver
Kathryn Beeler
Michelle Bemmann
Elizabeth Bittson
Nelle Bordeaux
Lynn Brennan
Katie Britt
Shannon Buck
Teresa Campbell
Erinn Carter
Ana Barisa Casanova
Daria Cetti
Elizabeth Christmas
Jennifer Claiborne
Jennifer Claron
Cheryl Clephane
Clair Craver
Ashton Daley
Allison Davis
Maria Davis
Keller Deal
Sarah Demaree
Lauren Denmark
Catherine Duncan
Mary Eady
Christine Earl
Catherine Edwards

Linda Elliott
Claudia Emmert
Melanie Finnegan
Carey Ford
Ansley Fox
Carey Fredrich
Jennifer Friedman
Yuntalay Gadson
Tanya Glaize
Jennifer Grafton
Brooke Guerra
Laura Haslam
Jennifer Hastie
Elizabeth Hausauer
Erica Herndon
Nicklaus Hogan
Nathasha Holmes
Jessi Horne
Tiffany Hughes
Lachlan Collins Ivy
Anne Jacobson
Jan Johnson
Emily Jones
Sarah Jones
Katie Joyner
Keller Kean
Mary Kerdasha
Jenny Lambeth
Kathy Ledvina
Carrie Lewis
Beth Longley
Amanda Love
Brooke Lozier

Alison Mahoney
Allison Marrero
Lara Martino
Loren Mathews
Vickie Matthews
Michele Mazzei
Sarah McCallar
Emily McCarthy
Laura McKenzie
Rikki McMillan
Stephanie Meredith
Erica Merritt
Johnnie Ann Morris
Suzanne Moseley
Kristen Murphy
Jami Newland
Laura Nottingham
Jackie Ogden
Wendy Owens
Hilary Parry
Rosanne Perna
Melissa Peters
Chelsea Phillips
Kathryn Piasta
Claire Pickering
Eugenia Pierson
Sara Pitts
Samantha Pogorelsky
Lauren Powell
Penny Rafferty
Tammy Ray
Brandyn Reagan
Beth Respress

Amy Riesinger
Matt Roher
Katie Rudder
Jenny Rutherford
Taqwaa Saleem
Swann Seiler
Jackie Schott
Allie Smith
Michelle Smith
Rebecca Strawn
Deborah Strickland
Jane Strickland
Sara Jane Strickland
Sue Strickland
Beth Taylor
Rachel Taylor
Willa Thiess
Jessica Thomas
Kim Thomas
Kristy Thorstad
Joan Trefz
Catherine Wallace
Susan Wallace
Margaret Walton
Melissa Wedincamp
Beth Wells
Mallory Whatley
Kathy Whitehurst
Mrs. Selma Wilkes
Carrie Jane Williamson
Rachel Wilson
Ashley Yerkey

The committee gratefully acknowledges support from Ferguson Kitchen and Bath Supply and Fabrication Design Concepts, Inc. for their sponsorships of the "Sweets on the Squares" and "Low Country Boil" socials, respectively. Both of these get-togethers allowed friends and family to celebrate the development of On the Squares – Savannah Style *and enjoy a taste of the recipes within.*

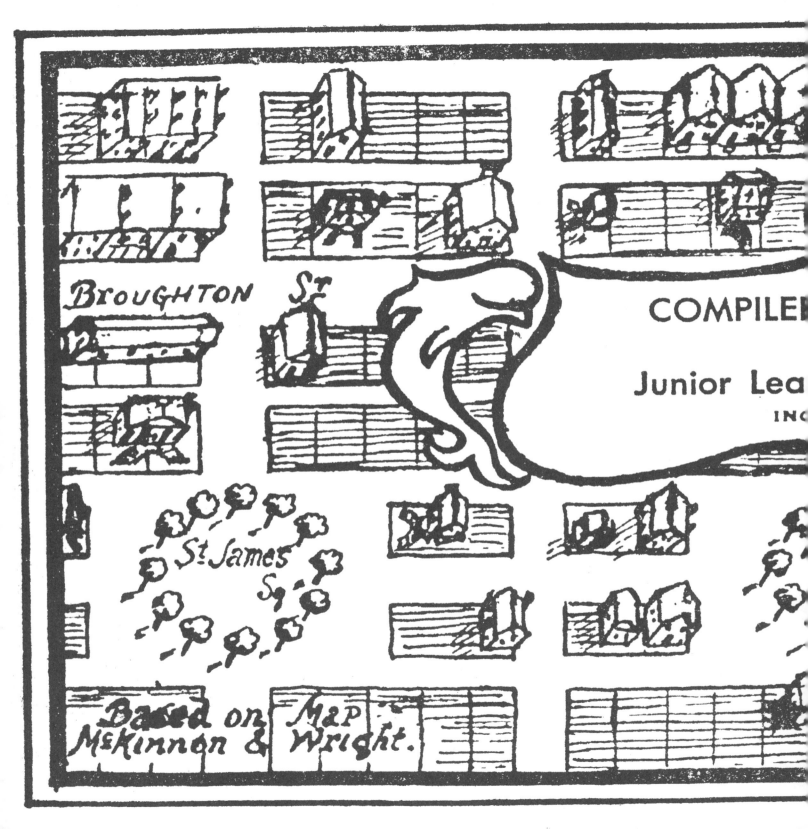

BROUGHTON St

COMPILE

Junior Lea

INC

St. James Sq.

Based on McKinnon & Map Wright.